★ ★ ★ ★ ★ ★ ★ ★ THE BOOK OF ★ ★ ★ ★ ★ ★ ★ ★

WILDLY SPECTACULAR
SPORTS
SCIENCE

★ ★

SEAN CONNOLLY

★ ★

WORKMAN PUBLISHING · NEW YORK

Library of Congress Cataloging-in-Publication Data is available.

ISBN 978-0-7611-8928-2

Design by Galen Smith

Cover by Galen Smith

Cover and interior illustrations by Chad Thomas

Photo research by Michael Di Mascio

Workman books are available at special discounts when purchased in bulk for premiums and sales promotions as well as for fund-raising or educational use. Special editions or book excerpts also can be created to specification. For details, contact the Special Sales Director at the address below, or send an email to specialmarkets@workman.com.

Workman Publishing Co., Inc.

225 Varick Street

New York, NY 10014-4381

workman.com

WORKMAN is a registered trademark of Workman Publishing Co., Inc.

Printed in the United States of America

First printing October 2016

10 9 8 7 6 5 4 3 2 1

To my family—and to all the scientists who were "good sports" along the way.

This book has been a labor of love from start to finish, but like most sporting—and scientific—achievements, it has been a team effort. My family provided support and confidence all through this process, often acting as playing partners, backstops, coaches, and teammates as the need arose.

I turn to New York City now to thank those who helped turn interesting ideas into these printed pages, in particular my agent, Jim Levine of the Levine Greenberg Rostan Literary Agency. Likewise I was fortunate to team up with Workman Publishing's two "Daniels": Daniel Nayeri, Director of Children's Publishing, for his inspired vision about the project from the very beginning, and editor Danny Cooper for his diligent and enthusiastic editing, patience, and practical suggestions. Designer Galen Smith and production editor Beth Levy were wonderfully creative and hardworking as well.

In addition, the following individuals and organizations have provided inspiration or assistance, and sometimes both: Berkshire Film & Video, Frank Ciccotti, Gregory Etter, Gary Hoffman, Kingswood School, Dr. Peter Lydon, M.I.T.'s Educational Studies Program, Robert Rauch, Peter Rielly, Jennifer Spohn, and Elizabeth Stell.

CONTENTS

On the Move Outside

INTRODUCTION

"DID YOU GET TICKETS FOR SATURDAY'S BIG game?"

"No, who's playing?"

"Nuclear physicists versus chemists, duh!"

That exchange probably sounds a bit ridiculous. Come on—physicists against chemists?! What are they going to do, race to tidy up a lab or stack a bunch of test tubes? But if you think it over, you'll find that even if scientists aren't competing directly in sports, most athletes are demonstrating science every day. And so are you, each time you wind up to pitch, skate the length of the rink, or take a turn on the trampoline.

A LONG TRADITION

Whether it's a gravity-defying slam dunk or a gymnast's landing that "nails it," athletes are using science all the time. Nowadays, many teams and individual athletes hire "sports scientists" to boost their performance, improve their diet, or just help them stay in shape—but the science has always been there.

Trial and error—a basic scientific method—helped ancient Greek discus throwers in the first Olympic Games nearly 3,000 years ago. Runners from that same era would soon have learned when to sprint and when to pace themselves, even if they didn't know about the chemistry of energy production.

It's only natural that this basic sense of curiosity—coupled with an equally natural desire to win—would draw technology (where science meets engineering) into the world of sport. Why give tennis balls a furry surface?

How does one type of putter help you master the two-putt out on the green? Would a racing car go faster if it had wings?

THE SPORTS . . .

The Book of Wildly Spectacular Sports Science gives you the chance to learn—or learn even more—about dozens of sports. And the world of sports really is wide and wild. Think of the nerves you'd need to launch yourself off a ski jump or "hang ten" on a monster wave. What about the superhero strength you'd require to chop wooden blocks with your bare hands, or the magical powers necessary to give a baseball a mind of its own as it dances the 60 feet, 6 inches to home plate?

But there's more to sports than being superhuman or wizardlike. What about the sports and physical activities you can do day in and day out? How about trying to get the hang of slacklining? Or learn how to make a soccer ball stop dead and drop to your feet so you can shoot or score? Or maybe try to figure out how some gears on your bike let you climb the steepest hill?

. . . AND THE SCIENCE BEHIND THEM . . .

Of course, it's science that provides the key to understanding most sports, from the familiar everyday variety to the ones that make you think, "Are they out of their minds trying to do that?!" In the following pages you'll find that there's a scientific explanation for each flip, jump, turn, and Hail Mary pass. It's great to see how classroom terms like momentum, center of mass, Newton's laws of motion, and friction have starring roles in the world of sports.

Plus, you'll come across a few terms for the first time: Do you think that the "moment of inertia" belongs with auto racing or golf? Does electrostatic friction help explain the bounciness of a trampoline or why you need to wax a snowboard? You'll soon find out.

The book's explanations—and your own experiments—don't just help you learn the scientific secret for one sport. They also show how these scientific principles connect one sport to another. Did you ever imagine that knowing how a knuckleball works would help you with soccer free kicks? Or that the best way to get "air" on a skateboard jump is to study a figure-skating routine? You'll find dozens of these links as you read the book.

HOW TO USE THIS BOOK

Each entry focuses on a sport—or to be precise, the science that gives that sport its character and excitement. The entries themselves are grouped into seven chapters based on something that their entries share. It could be something broad, like when or where the sports are played ("Winter Sports," "Indoor Sports"), or it could concentrate on how the sport is played ("Bat and Ball Sports," "Rackets and Clubs").

An entry begins with a reminder of what makes a particular sport so cool before setting the scene for the science that makes it all happen. And what better way to grasp that science than with an experiment? The chapter leads up to its experiment, which begins with an idea of how long it's going to take. You'll find lots of quick-fire experiments that get you a payoff in a couple of minutes. Others reveal their secrets over a longer stretch of time but are definitely worth the wait.

The experiment then breaks down into the following sections:

THE LINEUP

Here's the list of the ingredients you'll need to perform the experiment. Don't worry—you're sure to find pretty much everything in your house (and sometimes at the park).

PLAY BALL!

Okay, here you'll find the nuts and bolts of the whole thing. The numbered step-by-step instructions take you all the way through the experiment.

TWO-MINUTE WARNING

Special advice (and sometimes a safety warning) for the experiment.

SLO-MO REPLAY

The explanation of the science that lies at the heart of the experiment, along with a reminder of how it relates to that entry's sport.

FINAL WORDS

Okay, so you might not be hired as the new Denver Broncos QB after reading this book, and Harvard might need to interview a few other candidates for science-teaching posts. But you should be able to appreciate your favorite sports *and* science even more. No one needs to tell you to have fun when you go out to play, but can you imagine hearing your mom shouting, "I've called you five times already! Would you stop it with all that science—it's suppertime!"

Well, who knows? You might hear that after you look through this book.

CHAPTER ONE

BAT *and* BALL Sports

What better place to start a book on sports than with America's national pastime, baseball (and its close relatives, softball and Wiffle ball)? We're in "it's outta here!" territory—or was that "swing and a miss"? Either way, there's a lot of science at work, particularly if you're trying to figure out why one pitch will let you tee off while another will curve and drop right past you into the catcher's mitt.

You will likely see some of the scientific principles behind these sports cropping up again later in the book, in slightly different forms. But it's good to get started "right off the bat" by matching that science with sports you've probably played for as long as you can remember. That way, you might find that you don't have to deal with so many knuckleballs . . . but we can't promise.

HOW DOES A KNUCKLEBALL Work?

YOU'RE AT THE PLATE, HANDS GRIPPING THE bat and eyes on the ball as the pitcher delivers. You've got enough time to line up this meatball to send it flying, and you power into your swing. But a split second before you make contact, the ball dips to the left—five inches beneath your bat. *Strike one!* Two more pitches and two more swinging strikes follow. You've just been caught by the most devilish pitch in baseball: the knuckleball. Curveballs curve, sinkers sink, and fastballs go fast . . . but knuckleballs just can't be predicted. They seem to dip, wiggle, and stall, and no two pitches behave the same way. Plus, they're slower than a herd of snails stampeding through peanut butter. So what's the story?

IT'S NO DRAG

Baseball isn't the only sport featuring a ball with a mind of its own. Volleyball spikes and bowled cricket balls can outfox opponents because of their erratic movement. Cristiano Ronaldo, star forward for Real Madrid soccer club, regularly sends free kicks zigging and zagging past walls of defenders and into the net. The name he gives to this no-spin weapon? "The knuckleball." Scientists have gained a basic understanding of the knuckleball—a lack of spin makes its flight unpredictable. But why that happens is still a matter of study in physics labs. You can do a simple experiment to get an idea of just what makes the knuckleball such a devious pitch, all in the comfort of your kitchen.

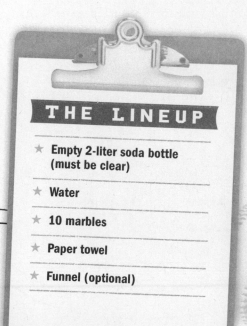

THE LINEUP

★ **Empty 2-liter soda bottle (must be clear)**

★ **Water**

★ **10 marbles**

★ **Paper towel**

★ **Funnel (optional)**

PLAY BALL!

 1 Fill the bottle to the very top with water and place it on a table or counter.

2 Find a position, crouched or sitting, where you can observe the bottle comfortably at eye level.

3 Hold a marble, pinched between forefinger and thumb, directly over the mouth of the bottle. The marble should almost touch the water.

 4 Release the marble, making sure that you don't let it spin out of your hand.

TWO-MINUTE WARNING

Make sure the water level is right up to the top of the bottle throughout the experiment. That way, the marble won't pick up any spin as it drops through the air into the water. Top up the level if it gets low and wipe the side of the bottle with the paper towel.

5 Observe the marble's path as it sinks.

6 Repeat Steps 3 to 5 with the other marbles. Can you get three in a row to go the same way?

SLO-MO REPLAY ▶

In this experiment, you're observing a basic scientific principle: Many forces behave similarly in gases and liquids. A knuckleball's flight through the air (a gas) is similar to the marble's path through the water (a liquid). You can see that no two "drops" were identical, just as no two knuckleball pitches are. A spinning ball (in curveballs, fastballs, and other pitches) channels air to one side. That channeling creates a consistent wake behind the ball, making the drag—the force that slows its forward movement—behave steadily. Without the spin, the knuckleball channels air this way and that depending on tiny variations in its movement. There's no consistent guidance, so the ball goes haywire. Sometimes it might even go where you expect it to—but don't count on it, slugger.

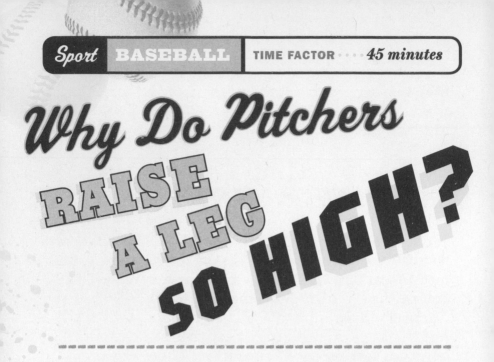

Why Do Pitchers RAISE A LEG SO HIGH?

"HE-E-E-RE'S THE WINDUP . . . AND THE PITCH . . . STEE-RIKE THREE!"

Whether it's Game 7 of the World Series or opening day of Little League season, those words describe some of the most suspenseful and dramatic moments in a baseball game. What makes it even more exciting is watching the pitcher lean way back, with his front leg stretched out and up, before unleashing that heat-seeking fastball. You might not have realized that with each delivery, the pitcher is performing a science demo of the principle known as torque. And that torque feeds into momentum, the force an object has when it moves—an object like a 95 mph fastball, for instance.

MEDIEVAL FASTBALL

Prepare to transport from the world of Major League fastballs to medieval fireballs. You're about to test a mechanical throwing arm by building a miniature trebuchet, the sort of throwing machine that terrified castle defenders. Back in the Middle Ages, soldiers attacked fortresses by heaving stones, dead or diseased animals, and even blazing fireballs over the walls. It took a lot of force to launch those heavy objects over great distances, and this experiment will show you how the attackers could maximize their force. Real trebuchets were about 30 feet tall and could launch a 300-pound rock about 300 yards—hey, don't get any crazy ideas!—but your smaller version works on the very same principles of torque and momentum, shedding light on how that outstretched leg helps a pitcher.

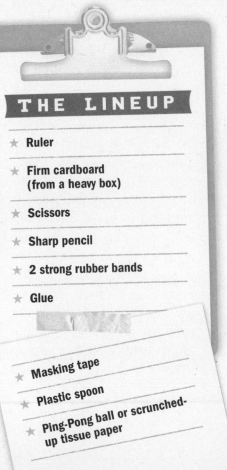

THE LINEUP

* Ruler
* Firm cardboard (from a heavy box)
* Scissors
* Sharp pencil
* 2 strong rubber bands
* Glue
* Masking tape
* Plastic spoon
* Ping-Pong ball or scrunched-up tissue paper

PLAY BALL!

1 Measure and cut out two pieces of cardboard—one 6 × 6 inches (the "base") and the other 2 × 6 inches (the "launcher").

2 Fold the launcher piece in half, so that each half measures 2 × 3 inches.

3 Use the pencil to punch a hole in the middle of each flap of the launcher.

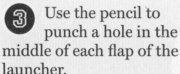

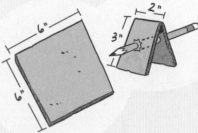

4 Line up the folded edge of the launcher with one edge of the base, at center.

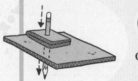

5 Mark and then punch a hole in the base, directly under the holes of the launcher.

6 Cut one rubber band and tie a knot in one end.

7 Feed the other end of the rubber band from below the base and through the two launcher holes. (The launcher should still be lined up along the edge of the base, with the flaps facing inward.)

8 Tie the other end of the rubber band so that there's just over an inch of slack between the two knots.

Glue the underside of the launcher onto the base and tape it with two pieces of masking tape as well.

 Unfold the launcher and tape the spoon onto it. The spoon will need to move with the launcher acting as a hinge, so make sure you leave a little space for the launcher to move freely.

 Now you're ready to fire. Holding the base firmly, pull the spoon back, load it with the Ping-Pong ball (or balled-up tissue paper), and fire.

 Try a few firings to get an average distance, then cut and remove the rubber band.

 Cut, knot, and feed the second band through (as you did in Steps 6 to 8), but this time leaving a shorter gap between the knots.

 Try some sample firings and compare the distances.

TWO-MINUTE WARNING You might find it easier to have a friend hold the base down while you load up and fire. And remember: no blazing fireballs!

During a windup, a pitcher's body-twist and leg-raise build up force, transferring energy to their throwing arm. When the leg starts to swing down, it transfers force into the pitcher's upper body and arm. By then it becomes a matter of increased momentum, which is the force of movement.

By tightening the rubber band in this experiment, you've loaded a lot more force into the trebuchet's throwing arm (the spoon), just as the leg kick adds more force into the pitcher's delivery. Isaac Newton gave us the law that force is made up of mass × acceleration (speed), or $F = m \times a$. The pitcher's windup, like the tightening band, is increasing the overall force (F). So, since you've increased the force, and the mass of the baseball or Ping-Pong ball remains the same, then the acceleration must go up, too. More speed means longer tosses of fireballs . . . and faster fastballs.

WHAT HAPPENS
When a Pitcher
"DOCTORS"
A BALL?

PITCHERS ABSOLUTELY LOVE LICKING THEIR fingers. Is it just a nervous tic? Leftovers from yesterday's sloppy joe? Or is there more to it? Well, the rules of baseball are clear about what pitchers can and can't do to a ball, and they *always* have to wipe any wet fingers on their uniform before throwing. Since the 1920s, it has been illegal to tamper with a ball (called "doctoring") to

PETEY'S PINE TAR

get pitches to break wildly and unpredictably. But pitchers have tried all kinds of ways to make a "spitball," like applying pine tar, grease, or tobacco juice (*gross!*), and even notching and scuffing the ball. So why risk ejection—and crossing over to the Dark Side—to doctor a ball? And just what happens with a doctored pitch?

SMOKIN' FASTBALL?

Most pitches form a gently curving path as the spinning baseball moves aside the air that it meets. But anything uneven or bumpy on the surface of the ball will affect its flight. A doctored ball begins spinning like a normal pitch, only the irregularity on its surface creates turbulence as it passes through the air. (Maybe you've experienced air turbulence when a plane ride turns bumpy.) This experiment uses a technique similar to that of a wind tunnel. That's where engineers test automobiles and airplanes to see how they are affected as they move through the air. Wind tunnels do the opposite—they move the air past the car or plane. Here you'll use rising smoke to show the flow of air and the turbulence caused by an object in its way.

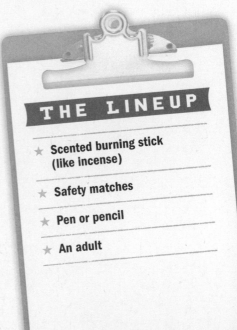

THE LINEUP

★ Scented burning stick (like incense)

★ Safety matches

★ Pen or pencil

★ An adult

PLAY BALL!

1 Find a spot where you can observe smoke, like next to a solidly colored wall (with no patterns).

2 Have an adult light the scented stick. Or (if no stick is available) light a match and blow it out.

3 Make sure the stick is held still, away from drafts, with the solid wall behind it.

4 Observe the smoke rising straight up and eventually spreading out after it travels a few inches.

TWO-MINUTE WARNING

Make sure you have an adult dealing with the burning stick and matches. If you can't find a scented stick, you can get the same effect from the smoke rising from a safety match that has been blown out. Long matches—the ones you use in fireplaces—produce smoke for longer than ordinary safety matches.

5 Hold the end of the pen or pencil in the first couple of inches of rising smoke.

6 Observe what happens to the smoke as it passes.

7 If you've used matches instead of a stick, repeat Steps 2 to 6 to get another good look.

SLO-MO REPLAY ▶▶

The straight movement of a liquid or gas is called a laminar flow. You get a laminar flow with rising smoke, or when you run water from a faucet. When that flow is disrupted, it goes in different directions and becomes a turbulent flow. Sometimes it regroups, but then it goes topsy-turvy again. The main thing to note is the unpredictable nature of the movement. The rising smoke is a laminar flow, but it becomes a turbulent flow when it hits the pencil or pen.

This experiment is a visual display of how a doctored baseball creates turbulence—and unpredictable motion—as it passes through the air on the way to the plate. You can see it swirling, jumping, and coming briefly back to its original path.

Just What *Is the* "SWEET SPOT"?

IT'S THE VERY FIRST AT BAT OF SOFTBALL season, and the perfect pitch is on the way—so you open up your stance, step into the swing, and . . . *YOUCH!!!* Foul ball. You drop your bat—your hands can't hold a thing. Was that an electric shock, or what?! Looks like you missed the "sweet spot," that bit of the bat that feels "right" when you make contact with the ball. And it's not just softball and baseball bats that have it—tennis and squash rackets, golf clubs, and anything else that hits a ball all have an area that's just right for making clean contact. It's all down to elastic matters. "Elastic" isn't just the rubber band you fling across the classroom, it's also an important concept in physics.

GOOD VIBRATIONS?

In physics terms, a ball hitting a bat is known as a collision, or "a meeting of objects in which each exerts a force upon the other, causing the exchange of energy or momentum." This exchange of energy is the key to the sweet spot. An elastic collision transfers kinetic energy (the energy of movement) during the exchange. The opposite type—an inelastic collision—absorbs some or all of that kinetic energy and converts it into other types of energy, like heat, sound, or in the unfortunate case of your stinging hands, vibrations. You experienced an inelastic collision by not making contact along the right part of the bat, which is a measly few inches long. That's the sweet spot: Hits feel good when you make solid contact there (no vibrations) and the kinetic energy can send the ball over the outfield fence. Elastic and inelastic collisions feature in lots of sports. Here's a chance to test some familiar objects to see how they stack up.

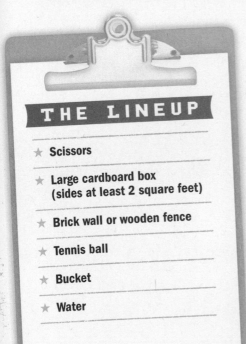

THE LINEUP

★ Scissors

★ Large cardboard box (sides at least 2 square feet)

★ Brick wall or wooden fence

★ Tennis ball

★ Bucket

★ Water

PLAY BALL!

 1 Cut the four upright sides of the box to create four rectangles or squares.

 2 Stack those four sides and lean the stack (almost upright) against a brick wall or wooden fence.

3 Stand about 10 feet back and throw the ball at half speed at the cardboard stack. Note how far back the ball bounces.

TWO-MINUTE WARNING

Make sure you perform these tests where you won't be making a mess or disturbing anyone. You're throwing the ball at half speed for a reason.

Remove one of the pieces of cardboard, restack, and repeat Step 3.

 Continue until you throw at the one remaining piece.

 Now throw the ball at the same speed directly at the wall or fence, again observing how far the ball bounces back.

⑦ Fill the bucket with water and throw the ball into it from 10 feet, observing what happens.

SLO-MO REPLAY ▷

This experiment is a great demonstration of elastic and inelastic collisions. Remember your hands stinging and the softball just skidding off the bat for a foul? Congratulations—you were demonstrating an inelastic collision. The kinetic force of the ball and bat transferred into vibrations that traveled into your hands.

You should be able to judge how elastic or inelastic each of the objects in this experiment is. In particular, what did you learn as you removed the layers of cardboard one by one? How about when the ball landed in the water—was it elastic or inelastic?

Why Is a WIFFLE BALL SO HARD TO HIT?

SURE, BASEBALL AND SOFTBALL ARE A BLAST to play, but Wiffle ball may have them beat. It's easy to organize (can't find nine players for each team? No problem!), you can play it pretty much anywhere, and you likely won't break any windows with your plastic equipment. But a scientific secret lurks behind the scenes.

We all know that it's really hard to hit the ball. Okay, so the yellow bat is half the width of a Louisville Slugger and the ball is coming at you at about 40 mph, less than half the speed of the "chin music" that major leaguers face every day. But the difficulty seems to come from the crazy flight of the ball once it's pitched. Forget about a pitchers' duel—we're talking a pitcher being cruel!

FLUID DELIVERIES

The key to a nasty Wiffle ball pitch lies in science—a special branch of physics, in fact, called fluid dynamics. It's all about the mechanics of fluids and the forces that act on them. But here's something to remember: "Fluids" don't just mean liquids; they also include gases. So when we talk about a Wiffle ball's path through the air (which is a gas), we're really talking about its path through a fluid. Some of the turns and dips in a Wiffle ball's path are the same as those of a baseball or soccer ball traveling through the air. But it's those holes in the ball—and the movement of the air inside them—that make all the difference, as you'll see with this simple demonstration.

THE LINEUP

★ Scissors

★ Duct tape

★ Wiffle ball

★ Friend to help you

PLAY BALL!

1 Cut two long pieces of duct tape and wrap them around the ball so that all of the holes are covered.

2 Ask a friend to be the catcher, about 15 paces from you.

3 Throw 10 pitches—some of them curveballs (flicking your throwing hand right or left on delivering).

4 Judge how easy it was for you to control the pitches and for the catcher to track them.

5 Now remove the tape to expose the holes.

TWO-MINUTE WARNING Conduct this experiment outside where you have a bit of space.

6 Repeat Steps 3 and 4.

7 The second batch of pitches should show a lot more movement.

SLO-MO REPLAY ▷

Let's start with the taped-up Wiffle ball, which is acting more like a "normal" ball. Two elements come into play. First: As it flies through the air, the ball usually spins, triggering something called the Magnus effect. That means that some air sticks to the surface of the ball and spins along with it. Friction slows down this air, meaning that the air on the other side of the ball moves faster.

This leads to the second element at play, known as Bernoulli's principle. It tells us that a fluid (air in this case) loses some pressure as it gains speed. So the air on the "faster" side of the ball has less pressure than the air on the slow side, pushing the ball toward that weaker side. That's why curveballs move away from the leading side. All this is true of "normal" balls—or your taped-up Wiffle ball. But all bets are off once those pesky holes come into play. That's because the air inside the ball has a mind of its own, swirling in circular currents called vortices (the singular is "vortex"). Depending on the speed of the Wiffle ball, these vortices can suddenly strengthen—or temporarily eliminate—the straight movement of the ball.

CHAPTER TWO

GOALS and FIELD GOALS

 I f you're running the entire length of the field to score a goal or touchdown, dodging a dozen or so tackling opponents along the way, you'll probably need a bit of help. Luckily, that help comes in the form of some familiar household ingredients, all in the name of science.

You can even use a DVD to learn how to throw a game-winning Hail Mary pass. Or use a golf ball to demonstrate why linemen are so enormous. Super Bowl champions often break open a bottle of champagne after the big game—why not use another celebration standby (a party balloon) to see how one NFL team *might* have fiddled with footballs on the way to Super Bowl XLIX?

A hulking football lineman can stop a running back in his tracks, but a wiry soccer midfielder can make a bullet pass fall gently at her feet. Hmm . . . more science? Yep, moving balls—and people—are subject to the same scientific laws. Even that wicked lacrosse shot, which seems to be part meteor and part flamethrower? Yessirree. You'll find out how in the most unlikely spot: your local playground.

WHY THROW FORWARD PASSES IN A SPIRAL?

IT'S 3RD AND 10 ON YOUR OWN 22-YARD LINE with the clock running out, and your team is down by five points. Just enough time for a miracle Hail Mary

pass to steal the win! The QB drops back, dodges two tackles, and somehow uncorks a tightly spinning pass that travels well beyond everyone—all except the star wide receiver, who hauls it in and sprints into the end zone for a glorious game-winning touchdown. Just about everything in that miraculous play depended on good luck—dodged tackles, the receivers getting open, the QB spotting them—except for one thing: No one in their right mind would consider throwing a football in anything other than a spiral. So what is it that makes the spiral the ideal throw? After all, baseball pitchers have a whole array of deliveries and grips. It's not rocket science, is it?

TESTING THE ROTATION

In fact, there *is* a bit of rocket science to explain why spiral passes work so well. Like rockets, planes, and cars, footballs need to cut down drag—the friction caused by air resistance as they move forward. That's why superfast objects like rockets and fighter planes have streamlined designs, with narrow fronts to cut through the air more easily. The football has two pointy ends, and either of them can act like the nose cone of a rocket as it tries to minimize drag. But how does it stay in that position through its entire flight, without drifting into a tumble? Meet a QB's best friend: angular momentum, or the amount of motion of a rotating object. Angular momentum keeps the object spinning along its axis and holds that axis in the same direction. (It's why you stay upright on a bike as long

THE LINEUP

★ Ballpoint pen

★ Large table or smooth floor

★ Poster putty

★ DVD (or Blu-ray Disc, CD, or video game disc)

as you're moving—the angular momentum of the spinning wheel works to keep the wheel upright. With less speed, you lose angular momentum and the bike tips.) And as long as that football's spinning, its nose is cutting a drag-beating path through the air. This experiment is a

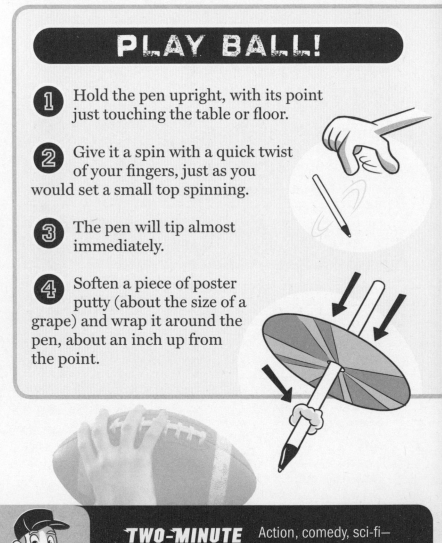

PLAY BALL!

1. Hold the pen upright, with its point just touching the table or floor.

2. Give it a spin with a quick twist of your fingers, just as you would set a small top spinning.

3. The pen will tip almost immediately.

4. Soften a piece of poster putty (about the size of a grape) and wrap it around the pen, about an inch up from the point.

TWO-MINUTE WARNING Action, comedy, sci-fi— the type of movie doesn't matter, but don't use someone's precious new DVD!

simple way to demonstrate angular momentum in just a few seconds. Think of the pen as the axis (like the imaginary line connecting the pointed ends of the football).

5 Hold the pen just between the point and the putty and slide the DVD down from the other side.

6 Press the DVD onto the putty so that it's even and secure.

7 Repeat Steps 1 and 2—the pen should spin and stay upright.

SLO-MO REPLAY ▶

Angular momentum depends on three elements—mass, velocity, and the object's radius. The radius is the distance from the center of a circle (like a DVD) to the edge of the curve. The pen on its own had too small a radius to create much angular momentum. You couldn't really increase its mass (making it heavier) or its velocity (spinning it much faster), but you were able to increase its radius by adding the DVD.

The football has more mass and a much longer radius than a pen, and quarterbacks practice getting a good spin (velocity) on their throws. It all adds up to angular momentum, which in turn keeps that pointed end facing forward and cutting down drag. Touchdown!

WHY ARE
LINEMEN SO
BIG?

THE FIVE MEMBERS OF THE OFFENSIVE LINE— a center, two guards, and two tackles—have just two main responsibilities. On running plays, they try to create holes in the defensive line so their runner can break through. And on passing plays, they protect the quarterback from being sacked. The four members of the defensive line do the exact opposite of their O-line counterparts: plugging gaps to stop runners and disrupting or even tackling the quarterback. But the two lines share something gigantic in common. They're big— *really* big. Linemen are heavier, taller, and usually slower than any other players. Is there a scientific reason why that sort of person is best for the job? Could someone smaller (and maybe nimbler) be successful?

HOLD THAT LINE!

Sir Isaac Newton, a genius physicist who lived in England about 300 years ago, wouldn't have known a running back from a cheerleader, but he could have told you that a lineman should always be "big," or to be more precise, "massive." That's because mass (the amount of matter in an object) plays a big part in the three laws of motion that he published in 1686. The second law states that a force (F) is a product of something's mass (m) multiplied by its acceleration (a). Or, as it usually appears in equation form, $F = m \times a$. Linemen need a lot of force to do their job, so if their mass is big then so is the force that they can generate. Meanwhile, acceleration is the amount that velocity changes. And if you multiply mass (m) by velocity (v), you get momentum (usually abbreviated "p"): $p = m \times v$. Momentum is often described as "force in motion," which is what your linemen need. They're not speed demons,

THE LINEUP

★ Smooth board or piece of stiff plastic (about 1 × 3 feet)

★ Hardcover book (roughly 160 pages)

★ 10 paperback books of about the same size (roughly 200 pages each)

★ Golf ball

★ Baseball

and they line up close to the ball anyway, so the "a" and the "v" aren't going to be too big. But to knock down—or withstand—the opposing line, they need a whole lot of momentum. You can get a handle on momentum in the following experiment.

PLAY BALL!

 Lay the board down on a flat surface such as a table or the floor.

 Stand the hardcover book at one end of the board, flush against the narrow side.

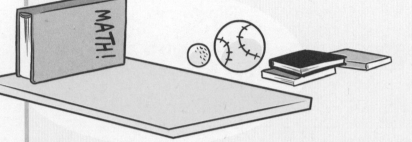

3 Slide one paperback flat under the far end of the board to create a slight slope down to the hardcover.

4 Set the golf ball just above the paperback and let it roll down to the other end.

5 If the hardcover stays upright, slide a second paperback under the board and repeat Step 4.

6 Keep adding paperbacks (making the slope steeper) until the golf ball knocks the hardcover down.

7 Repeat Steps 2 to 6 using the baseball instead of the golf ball.

SLO-MO REPLAY ▶

A baseball weighs about 150 grams, compared to the golf ball's nearly 50 grams. Eventually both managed to have enough momentum to knock the hardcover over, but they did it with different combinations of mass and velocity. You needed to get much more of a slope (increasing the velocity) for the golf ball to succeed. The baseball, with three times the mass, needed far less velocity.

Think about where the linemen line up. They're about as close as you can get to the ball, so they don't need much velocity to reach the action. But they do need momentum. Just like the baseball in this experiment, they rely on their mass.

Why WOULD A QUARTERBACK DEFLATE A FOOTBALL?

BEFORE WINNING SUPER BOWL XLIX IN A thrilling finish, the New England Patriots beat the Indianapolis Colts in the AFC Championship game on January 18, 2015. But it was a Colts interception in the first half that began the scandal known as "Deflategate." After star linebacker D'Qwell Jackson intercepted a pass from Patriots quarterback Tom Brady, a Colts equipment manager wound up with the ball, which he felt was under-inflated. He then measured it, finding it below the minimum 12.5 psi (pounds per square inch) required for game balls, and informed NFL officials. But why would a team "bend the rules" and lower the pressure in its football? And would it be worth all the hubbub and hullabaloo if a team did so deliberately? You can examine the problem the way a scientist would: empirically (through observation and record-keeping).

JUST A LOT OF COLD AIR?

The NFL rules clearly state that a game ball must be inflated to a pressure between 12.5 and 13.5 psi. Pumping up a football is like pumping a bike tire: It gets bigger and harder as the pressure increases. A ball that's a bit underinflated is easier to grasp and hold, giving an advantage in throwing, catching, and preventing fumbles. So you can see why a team might be tempted to underinflate its 12 allotted game balls. But things aren't so simple—air, like any gas, changes pressure as the surrounding temperature changes. You'll get a chance to observe both of these aspects of the mysterious "Deflategate" case in this experiment.

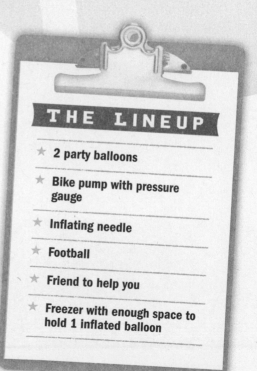

THE LINEUP

★ 2 party balloons

★ Bike pump with pressure gauge

★ Inflating needle

★ Football

★ Friend to help you

★ Freezer with enough space to hold 1 inflated balloon

PLAY BALL!

1. Blow up the balloons, tie them shut, and put one in the freezer (keeping the other nearby), noting the time.

2. Use the bike pump and inflating needle to blow the football up to 13.5 psi.

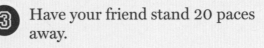

3. Have your friend stand 20 paces away.

4. Throw each other five passes, noting how many were caught.

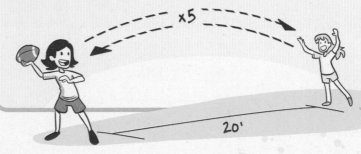

TWO-MINUTE WARNING If you can't find a friend to help pass the football, you could hang a cloth from a tree branch to act as a target. And no tackling!

5 Insert the needle to let some air out, and measure to try to reach 13 psi. (If you go too far just blow it back up a little.)

6 Repeat Steps 3 and 4.

7 Continue lowering the pressure by 0.5 psi (and repeating Steps 3 and 4) until you get to 10 psi.

8 Note which pressure produced the best control and the most complete passes.

9 After one hour, remove the balloon from the freezer.

10 Compare the sizes of the two balloons.

SLO-MO REPLAY ▷

Scientists would describe this experiment as an empirical study because it relies on hands-on observation. You're judging for yourself whether a slightly deflated football is easier to throw, catch, and hold onto. We're not saying that the Patriots did anything wrong, of course.

And what about those two balloons? The one that spent an hour in the freezer probably came out a bit smaller. That's because gases—like the air inside the balloon—contract when the surrounding temperature gets colder. Some Patriots fans were quick to point out that the footballs were pumped with room-temperature air and then spent hours outside on a January day in frigid New England, so the psi decreased. You can draw your own conclusions . . .

HOW DO YOU TRAP A SOCCER BALL?

YOU'RE JUST OUTSIDE THE GOAL AREA, WAIT-ing for a corner kick from the far side. You know your role—collect the ball from the corner, gain control, and either shoot it or feed one of your teammates. "Two-touch soccer" is the name of the game. The ball sails high over the goalie, curving slightly as it soars straight to you. Here's the two-touch moment—*hallelujah, it's here!* Only . . . it bounces harmlessly off your foot and rolls to a defender, who clears it downfield. You did everything right except control the ball in that first touch. What went wrong? How does Carli

Lloyd make it look so easy whenever she traps the ball? How does Clint Dempsey manage it time after time? Maybe the easiest way to find out is to use the one part of your body that's "off limits" in soccer—your hands.

"CONSERVATION" PROJECT

If you watch a soccer player trap a ball—so that it stops "dead"—you'll see her draw her foot back just before the ball makes contact. Whether she knows it or not, she's using the law of conservation of momentum to do the job. Momentum is the "p" in the equation $p = m \times v$, with "m" standing for mass and "v" for velocity (which includes speed). The ball has all the momentum as it flies toward the player. This "conservation" business means that momentum can't be destroyed, only transferred to something else: the player's foot. This experiment demonstrates the same conservation of momentum, but using your hand instead of your foot. You should be able to get the hang of it quickly, but will you have the confidence to take on an egg?

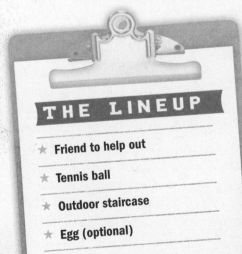

THE LINEUP

★ Friend to help out

★ Tennis ball

★ Outdoor staircase

★ Egg (optional)

PLAY BALL!

 Have your friend hold the ball about 2 feet above your outstretched hand.

 Let her drop the ball. Lower your hand just before you catch it.

TWO-MINUTE WARNING No doubt you'll catch the egg safely, having had all that practice with the tennis ball. But just in case, make sure you perform the experiment somewhere that's easy to clean up.

Try it until you can catch the ball confidently.

 Ask your friend to climb up a step, then repeat Steps 1 to 3.

 She should continue climbing, one step at a time, dropping the ball at each stop.

 Once she's reached the eighth step, have her replace the tennis ball with an egg—if you dare.

SLO-MO REPLAY ▶

A change in momentum is called an impulse, or the amount of force on an object multiplied by the time that a collision takes. If there's lots of force, then there's less time. Trapping the ball turns that on its head. By pulling her foot back, the player is increasing the amount of time that the "collision" takes. So with more time, there's less force. And that means less chance of the ball bouncing back off her foot.

You can find lots of examples of this principle all around you: Think of the soft, rubbery surface of playgrounds, especially near jungle gyms, swings, and other places where children could fall. Again, lengthening that time of impact can reduce the force—and the chance of injuries.

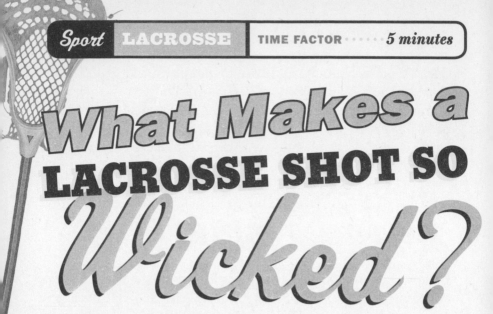

What Makes a LACROSSE SHOT SO Wicked?

LACROSSE MAY BE AN OLD SPORT—NORTH America's *oldest* traditional sport, in fact, dating back centuries to the first French settlers and the indigenous peoples before them—but it's anything but slow and boring. Players regularly fire shots that are 10 percent faster than a major leaguer's fastball, and from about half the

distance of a baseball pitch. Just what powers these monster shots, rifling in at up to 100 mph? The answer lies in some simple scientific properties, harnessed together to provide a real punch. You can experience these properties "from the inside" in one of the simplest experiments in this book.

GO FOR A SPIN

First of all, the lacrosse stick adds speed to what you could already do on your own. Your arm acts as a lever when you throw (actually two levers: shoulder-to-elbow and elbow-to-wrist). Each lever adds torque (rotational force), and the stick becomes a third lever. This lever combination would send the ball flying even if the player stood still and swung the stick directly over his head. However, he's also twisting his body back, creating what's called angular momentum, or its tendency to spin. Don't forget, momentum is mass multiplied by velocity, and all this coiling is building up the momentum in the stick. And here's the kicker: The player is usually running hard right up to the instant of shooting, transforming a so-so shot into a bona fide rocket blast. Find out how by making your way to the nearest playground.

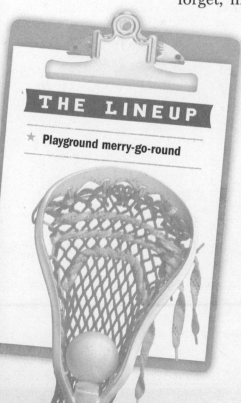

THE LINEUP

★ Playground merry-go-round

PLAY BALL!

 Find a local playground with a merry-go-round (the sort you push yourself, not one with horses).

 Give the merry-go-round a few pushes to make sure that it spins as it should.

 Make sure no one is on it and take about 20 paces back.

TWO-MINUTE WARNING Make absolutely sure that the playground has a soft "floor"—either soft, rubbery asphalt or sand—in case you take a tumble. This experiment requires concentration!

Run up to the merry-go-round at about half speed and jump on, holding tight. Note how many full spins you make.

 Repeat Step 4, gradually increasing your speed with each run until you reach full speed.

WEEEEEEEEEEEEEE!

CHAPTER THREE

Indoor Sports

Think of all the sports that you can play under cover. Not "undercover," as in detectives or spies (although it would be a blast to see them try to fake out some opponents), but sports that are played inside. And that's a pretty wide range, when you think about it.

This is an area of sports where magic seems to take over. How else could you explain a basketball player practically hovering in midair before scoring two points in the most dramatic way—a slam dunk? Or a judo competitor throwing an opponent who's twice her weight? And, while we're on the subject, how a karate expert chops through a stack of boards with his *bare hands*?!?

Of course, it's not magic, and you have a chance to look behind the curtain to see how these marvels are performed. Would you call them tricks? Techniques? Rocket science? Maybe that's getting closer to the answer.

CAN YOU REALLY Float in a Slam Dunk?

IT'S HARD TO IMAGINE THE FIRST GAME OF basketball, played in Springfield, Massachusetts, in 1891 and watched by its inventor, Dr. James Naismith. A peach basket hung 10 feet above the playing area with no backboard. Nearly all the players were under six feet tall, and scoring was so rare that the basket still had its base—

someone had to climb a ladder to get the ball down if a player *did* manage to score. Not exactly the Harlem Globetrotters! If Dr. Naismith were around today, he'd surely marvel at the players' speed, passing, shooting accuracy, and perhaps most of all, the slam dunk. He'd probably pinch himself if he saw players leaping up, hanging in midair for what seems like an eternity, and then slamming the ball *down* through the hoop. Now even modern spectators sometimes can't believe their eyes—or their memories. Did Michael Jordan really float like that? Did Dwight Howard really complete an alley-oop on a 12.5-foot-high rim? Did Candace Parker and Brittney Griner just throw it down, too? Holy jumpin' Toledo, what's going on around here?!

THE LINEUP

* 2 friends to help
* Small paperback book (about 5 × 7 inches and roughly 200 pages)
* Tennis ball
* Stopwatch or phone with timer
* Small hardcover book (similar size to the paperback)
* Large hardcover book (about 8 × 12 inches and roughly 300 pages)

JUST HANGIN' OUT

LeBron James, Kevin Durant, and Michael Jordan might tell you different, but the truth is that all these "high-fliers" are subject to the same laws of motion as the rest of us. The amount of time they spend in the air depends not on an ability to float but on the force of their jump, because a powerful jump will lead to more time in the air. Newton's laws of motion tell us that an object falls at the same rate that it rises. The time from the jump to the landing is called "hang time." Even the best players, jumping about three feet vertically, have a hang time of only about 0.85 seconds. They can use tricks, like tucking their legs up to make their jump seem higher, or holding onto the ball until they start coming down to make it seem as though they've been up longer. But nothing can

PLAY BALL!

1 Have one friend act as a timer while the other will be the "ball dropper."

2 Take the smaller paperback and prepare to use it to bat the tennis ball upward.

3 Ask the "ball dropper" to hold the ball high above your book. Your other friend should be ready to start timing.

TWO-MINUTE WARNING This is an outdoor experiment—you don't want to damage anything inside, plus you'd probably hit the ceiling and throw off your timing!

keep them airborne longer than our old buddy Newton would predict. This experiment won't get "tricky," but it will drive home the connection between upward forces and the length of hang time.

④ At the count of three, have the ball dropped. The timer should start when you hit the ball and stop when the ball lands.

⑤ Repeat Steps 2 to 4 with each of the other books in turn and note the different times.

SLO-MO REPLAY ▶

This is one of those "two for the price of one" experiments. The first is a comparison of the different momentums as you use each book. Remember that momentum is the result of mass × velocity. Assuming you swung each book at the same speed, you could say that the velocity was the same. But the mass increased with each book, so the momentum also rose.

Remember, too, that the key to slam-dunk success is hang time, and that all depends on the force of the jump sending the player higher. Well, increasing the force of each tennis ball "jump" in this experiment should have led to greater hang times (which your friend timed). Is that how it worked out?

Why Does PUMPING UP A Basketball MAKE IT BOUNCIER?

NOT ALL BALLS ARE THE SAME SIZE, SO IT isn't very surprising that there are different levels of bounciness. Imagine if Ping-Pong balls bounced only as much as croquet balls, or picture playing bizarro-tennis with something that bounced as much as a baseball. Spare a thought for the Aztecs, who played a sacred ball game using human heads! But few sports rely on the

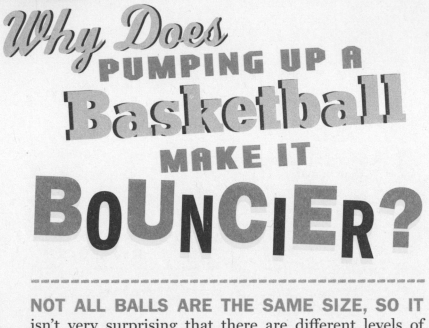

bounciness of the ball as much as basketball. Dribbling, rebounds, and bounce passes depend on it entirely (not to mention a trick shot or two). Let's find out how the sport gets the biggest bounce from its main player: the ball.

GETTING YOUR BOUNCE BACK

Here's another chance to do an empirical experiment (that's the sort that relies closely on observation). We all know that basketballs need to be filled with air. They're a bit like balloons, really, except their "skin" is a lot tougher. Make sure you watch very closely and mark exactly where you observe the ball's movement—and where it stops. And don't read the "Slo-Mo Replay" until you've recorded your own measurements! You don't want an expected result in the back of your mind to affect your experiment. (Hint: That result is the NBA's recommended pressure for basketballs.)

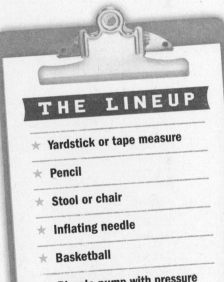

THE LINEUP

★ Yardstick or tape measure

★ Pencil

★ Stool or chair

★ Inflating needle

★ Basketball

★ Bicycle pump with pressure gauge (or pump and gauge separately if the pump has no gauge)

★ Paper or notebook

PLAY BALL!

1 Find a wall or door frame that you can mark with a pencil (without getting into trouble).

2 Measure and mark a spot that's exactly 6 feet up from the floor. You might find it easier to stand on a stool or chair.

3 Insert the needle into the basketball and let it deflate almost fully.

TWO-MINUTE WARNING You'll need to perform this experiment somewhere that has a hard, smooth floor (not carpeted) because you want the best bounce. Be careful if you're doing it outside, where pebbles or uneven asphalt can produce crooked bounces.

4 Connect the pump and check the air pressure of the basketball. Continue pumping until it reads 5 pounds per square inch (psi).

 5 Remove the needle and hold the ball so that the bottom of it lines up with the 6-foot mark.

 6 Let the ball fall and observe how high it bounces back, noting this measurement on your paper or in the notebook.

 7 Repeat Steps 4, 5, and 6 for increasing pressures: 6, 7, 8, and 9 psi.

SLO-MO REPLAY ▶

As you can tell, inflating the ball increases the air pressure inside. That's because of Boyle's law, which states that the pressure of a gas increases if it's squeezed into a smaller volume—or if more of the gas is squeezed into the same volume. The extra pressure inside the ball applies a force to any surface that it hits (the floor or ground in this experiment). And that's where Newton's third law of motion has its say: For every action, there is an opposite and equal reaction. That reaction is the bounce. So it makes sense that the bounce gets bigger as the pressure inside (from inflation) increases.

The NBA calls for their basketballs to be inflated to 7.5 to 8.5 psi, with most falling right in the middle (8 psi). And dropped from a height of 6 feet, as in this experiment, the top of the ball should bounce back to a height of 47 to 55 inches.

How Can You THROW A HEAVIER OPPONENT?

A WIRY YOUNG WOMAN HEARS SOME SHUF-fling footsteps in the shadows, then sees a hulking shape—a young man who's a good head taller and built like a tank. Before you know it, he's grabbed the bag from her shoulders. Chuckling, he starts to push her away. But suddenly there's a shuffle, and the man's arm is over the

woman's shoulder. Quick as a flash there's a twist, a turn, and he's swung up and over the woman. *Thump!* He's on the ground, winded and dazed but otherwise unhurt. The woman picks up her bag, zips it shut, and walks on, turning back once to say, "Don't mess with anyone who does judo."

IF I HAD A HAMMER

Whether they're performing kicks, holds, or throws, judoka (people who do judo) constantly use scientific principles to gain an advantage in their sport. One of the most common is the concept of center of mass, or "the point in a body at which the mass is considered to be concentrated." You don't need to be a scientist or judoka to work with this principle—just try standing on one foot. Sometimes you sway a little this way and that to stay upright. You're actually making sure that your center of mass is concentrated over your support (the one foot on the ground). Judoka try to move their opponents so that their center of mass is no longer over their feet, which anchor them, letting gravity and torque do all the work. That's how the young woman was able to throw her much bigger attacker. Try this cool experiment to get an idea of how center of mass sometimes seems a little weird, even though you know it makes perfect sense.

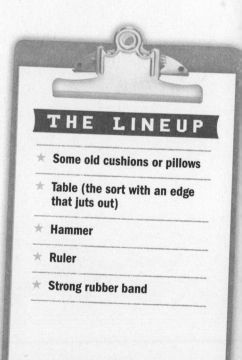

THE LINEUP

★ Some old cushions or pillows

★ Table (the sort with an edge that juts out)

★ Hammer

★ Ruler

★ Strong rubber band

Arrange the cushions or pillows below the edge of the table.

 Hold the hammer next to the ruler so that the handle end of the hammer aligns with the end of the ruler.

3 Slide the rubber band up from that end so that it goes around both the hammer and the ruler; stop about an inch before the head of the hammer.

4 Holding the hammer and ruler together—and keeping the ends of each touching—slide the other end of the ruler about an inch

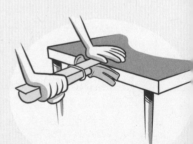

TWO-MINUTE WARNING Make sure to position the cushions directly below the hanging (and possibly falling) hammer: You don't want to break floor tiles, do you? (Okay, don't answer that question.)

along the top of the table. Hold it pressed in place with your other hand.

5 The hammer will be hanging, held up by the rubber band (near the head), and with your hand holding it to the far end of the ruler (on the other end).

GO SLOW!

6 Slowly remove both hands—the ruler should remain jutting out from the table with the hammer hanging beneath it.

7 Be patient: Most people need to try this several times before they get it to work.

SLO-MO REPLAY ▶

Like some of the best experiments, this one takes a concept and flips it on its head. You know from the judo example that manipulating center of mass (roughly in the middle of the man's chest) can make a stable object unstable. You're doing the opposite—making an unstable combination stable—with clever use of the center of mass.

In a regularly shaped object that has an even density (like an ice cube), the center of mass is exactly in the middle. With irregular shapes or combinations of objects, it can sometimes be outside either object. You know that the metal head of the hammer is much denser than the wooden handle, so you need more of the handle to balance the head's extra mass. The hammer's center of mass is right where the long handle meets the shorter (but denser) head. That's why it looks lopsided even though it's balanced.

CHOPPING WOOD WITH YOUR BARE HANDS?

IT'S ONE OF THE MOST EYE-CATCHING—AND scariest—sights in sport. A martial arts expert, dressed in loose white clothing, walks up to a stack of wooden boards positioned between two columns of cinder blocks. The audience goes silent as he steps forward, cocks an arm back, and *THWOOK*—slams his open hand down

vertically onto the stack. The boards split in two and go flying. That's it! No ax. No saw. Just a bare hand splitting the stack of wood. How the heck can he do that? Maybe the white martial arts outfit doubles as a lab coat, because that unbelievable chop is really a demonstration of momentum (the force of movement), Newton's second law of motion (force equals mass × acceleration), and density (the amount of weight, or mass, in a given space, or volume). You can harness those elements yourself with a neat chopping experiment. You may become a sensei in no time, young grasshopper.

KARATE KIDDING AROUND

The Japanese word *tegatana* ("hand sword") describes the martial arts blow that we usually call a karate chop. It can be used to strike—or block—in combat as well as to break menacing-looking stacks of wood or bricks. Okay, so no one's going to get hurt with this experiment, but it really does give you an idea of how martial arts masters manage to pull off those mighty chops. You'll build a bridge of Popsicle sticks across a gap between two bricks or books of similar size. If you use books instead of bricks, make sure they're hardcover. Something too soft will absorb some of the force of your blow—instead of your target.

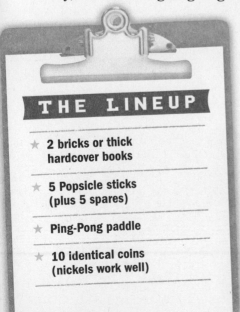

THE LINEUP

★ 2 bricks or thick hardcover books

★ 5 Popsicle sticks (plus 5 spares)

★ Ping-Pong paddle

★ 10 identical coins (nickels work well)

PLAY BALL!

1 Position two bricks about 2½ inches apart on a hard floor or table. If you're using books, make sure they're level.

2 Place a Popsicle stick so that it spans the gap, with about the same length resting on each brick or book pile.

3 Add four more sticks so that you have a pile five sticks high. Make sure they're lined up accurately.

4 Hold the paddle above the sticks and give a firm strike downward. (It should be firm but not too strong.)

5 The sticks probably bounced around and off, but didn't break.

TWO-MINUTE WARNING Do not—repeat, *DO NOT*—try to karate-chop piles of wood, logs, or bricks. Those martial-arts experts may look as cool as cucumbers, but some of them have also learned a lot about living through pain . . . and recovering from painful broken bones. Just stick to this comparatively "hands-off" version.

Begin stacking them again, putting a coin under each side of the bottom stick where it rests on the brick or book.

 Continue stacking, adding another coin on each side at each level.

 You should finish with another five-stick-high pile, with coin "spacers" separating the layers.

Repeat Step 4. This time you should be able to break some or even all of the sticks.

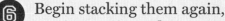

SLO-MO REPLAY ▶

Before you say, "Okay, this works with Popsicle sticks, but those guys use *real* wood," remember that demonstrations use soft or brittle wood, which snaps more easily. Even cinder blocks or bricks—other popular "targets"— will snap if they're hit right. Have you ever seen someone karate-chop marble or a steel bar? Didn't think so. But your demo shared something with most real examples. Your coins acted as spacers between the sticks, so instead of breaking a single bundle of sticks, you did it one by one.

Most of the real karate displays use spacers in this way, too. It's all about reducing the overall density of the sticks to make chopping all of them easier. A little bit of your downward momentum was used up breaking the first stick, and a little bit more for the second, and so on . . . but you still had enough to break them all. Think about how much easier it is to snap 10 twigs one by one than it is if you hold them all tightly together.

How Do Trampolines GIVE THAT BOUNCE?

WE'VE ALL HAD A BLAST BOUNCING ON trampolines—going for altitude records, twisting and turning in midair, or even pretending to be weightless astronauts. But did you know this simplest of activities is really a physics lab in action? With anything involving motion, gravity, springs, and solids, there's bound to be some very illuminating scientific explanations. Can you see that man dressed in a long overcoat and breeches, bouncing up and down with a broad grin on his face? Look—his long, curly wig has flown off! Well, perhaps that's all in the realm of imagination: It's unlikely that Sir Isaac Newton ever set foot on a trampoline, or even heard of one. But his scientific work described exactly how a trampoline works, as you'll see for yourself.

"ELASTIC" COLLISIONS

It's funny how the terms "elastic collision" and "inelastic collision" trouble some people. Many a young scientist wonders: How can something hard like a baseball bat or golf club be elastic in any way? Well, an elastic collision is a collision of objects that preserves a lot of its original kinetic (movement) energy, like a basketball dribbled off a gym floor. An inelastic collision loses that energy, like when you throw a baseball at a pillow. You're about to make a trampoline, and you'll see all of Newton's laws of motion at work in your own kitchen.

NEWTON

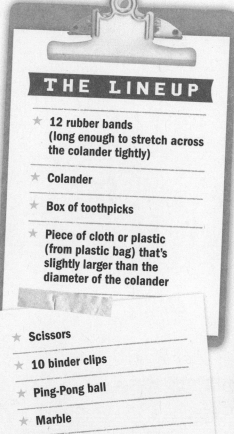

THE LINEUP

* 12 rubber bands
  (long enough to stretch across the colander tightly)

* Colander

* Box of toothpicks

* Piece of cloth or plastic
  (from plastic bag) that's slightly larger than the diameter of the colander

* Scissors

* 10 binder clips

* Ping-Pong ball

* Marble

* Golf ball

* Tennis ball

* Ruler

PLAY BALL!

1 Feed a rubber band through one of the holes at the top of the colander.

2 Slide a toothpick down inside the loop that juts out.

3 Feed the other end through the hole on the opposite side and secure it with another toothpick. The rubber band should be taut.

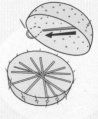

4 Continue feeding all of the rubber bands evenly across the colander.

5 Place the cut piece of cloth or plastic on the rubber bands, stretched tight, and secure it with the binder clips. You now have your trampoline.

TWO-MINUTE WARNING You can perform this experiment either inside or outside, but wherever you do it, make sure to clear away things that could break.

6 Starting with a Ping-Pong ball—then a marble, a golf ball, and a tennis ball—drop objects of increasing weight (mass) onto the trampoline from a height of 18 inches.

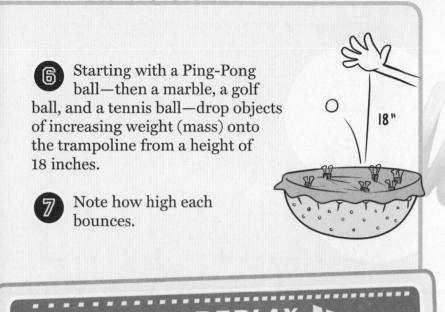

7 Note how high each bounces.

SLO-MO REPLAY ▶

There's a lot of cool science at work here. For starters, there's Newton's first law, which tells us that an object will stay at rest (or in motion) unless an outside force acts on it. So the marble and Ping-Pong ball were at rest in your hand until you let go and the force of gravity acted on them.

Next up, the second law tells us that the mass and acceleration of the falling object would determine its force. That meant that the heavier object (more mass) hit the trampoline with more force. This hitting (or collision) triggered Newton's third law: For every action there is an opposite and equal reaction. The "bounce" on the trampoline is that opposite force, and it's also where the "elastic" bit came in.

An elastic collision conserves all—or most—of the kinetic (movement) energy. If the objects fell onto sand or mud, the collision would be inelastic because the kinetic energy wasn't transferred. But with a bouncy trampoline, up things go, until an opposite force (gravity) pulls them back down, where they get *another* opposite force. So why doesn't this go on forever? Because some of the force of each collision spills out in vibrations (notice how the whole trampoline shakes?), and some gets converted into heat from friction as things travel through the air.

How Do *Gymnasts* "STICK IT"?

GYMNASTICS CALLS FOR PHYSICAL FITNESS, split-second timing, artistry, and a whole lot of bravery. Whether they're performing floor routines, swinging on parallel bars and rings, or springing off of vaults, gymnasts are constantly analyzing friction and momentum to make lightning-fast scientific decisions: "Will beginning my twist straight off make me over-rotate?" "Is there enough room on the diagonal to let me do three flips?" "Will tuck position be too fast for my double back?" Yowza! One of the most jaw-dropping skills in gymnastics is to "stick it," the ability to stop absolutely stock-still at the end of the routine. How do they manage it, after all that amazing movement? Any mortal being would flip right over!

DREAM ENDING

You sprint down the runway at top speed—over 15 mph—to build up momentum. You launch toward the vault, arms curved in to act as an uncoiling spring when you hit (the same science as a trampoline—adding even more strength to the opposite and equal force of impact as you push off). Then you sail up as high as 13 feet, still moving forward as you harness forces for your twists and flips. One last flip well past the vault, and you're heading down faster than a jackrabbit. *Boom!* You've just nailed it: legs together on impact, with no extra steps. Just stick it and wait for the applause. . . . Well, okay, that was last night's dream. Today, you work on that sticking-it routine, only you're in the kitchen rather than the gym. Time to use some science!

THE LINEUP

* Kitchen chair
* Newspaper
* Cushions from a sofa or easy chair

PLAY BALL!

 Place the chair in the middle of the kitchen, with at least 6 feet of floor space in front of it.

 Spread some newspaper on the floor in front of the chair. (This keeps the cushions clean.)

 Set the cushions on the newspaper, about 2 or 3 feet in front of the chair.

 Stand on the chair, facing the cushions.

 Jump up and out and don't bend your knees as you land on the cushions: Aim to stick it by staying perfectly still.

TWO-MINUTE WARNING

It's possible—but unlikely—that you could take a tumble on one of your jumps, so focus and be careful. Make sure there's nothing delicate or breakable anywhere near the chair, and take care that there's nothing nearby that could hurt you.

6 Repeat Steps 4 to 5 but land with your knees bent.

7 Remove the cushions and repeat Steps 4 to 5, once with unbent knees and once with bent.

8 Work out which of the four efforts was most successful.

SLO-MO REPLAY ▶▶

The landing is a demonstration of the science concept called impulse, which describes the change in momentum. Impulse is the product of impact force multiplied by impact time (how long it takes to land). The force of impact can unsettle the gymnast's landing, making it much harder to "stick it." Since the impulse is the same in each jump, you can reduce the force by lengthening the impact time. Landing on the soft cushions, coupled with bending your knees, will do just that. Was that the combination that made it easiest to stick it in this experiment?

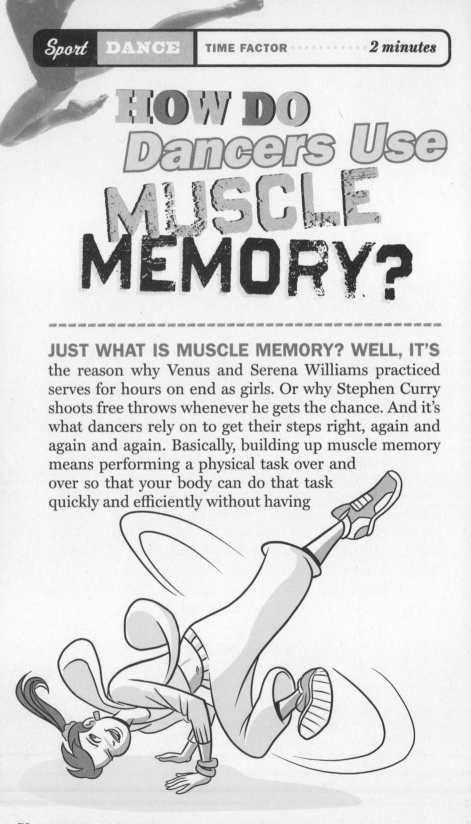

HOW DO Dancers Use MUSCLE MEMORY?

JUST WHAT IS MUSCLE MEMORY? WELL, IT'S the reason why Venus and Serena Williams practiced serves for hours on end as girls. Or why Stephen Curry shoots free throws whenever he gets the chance. And it's what dancers rely on to get their steps right, again and again and again. Basically, building up muscle memory means performing a physical task over and over so that your body can do that task quickly and efficiently without having to think too much about it. Can you ride a bike? If so, you've used muscle memory. When you were learning, you had to think about all sorts of things—how to grip the handlebars, how fast to pedal, where to put your toes and heels, and so on. But now you can do those things without even thinking—or falling!

𝕳𝕬𝕹𝕯𝕾 𝖀𝕻!

When you perform a new physical movement, your brain learns complicated sets of instructions that it sends out to muscles in different parts of your body—but all in the right order. A complicated action, such as a ballroom dance routine, is actually a series of separate actions sequenced just so: "Lead with the left, then the right, then turn, back again, over, back, right arm up, then down, and again." Phew! Getting one of those wrong, or doing it in the wrong order, can throw you (and your dance partner) off completely. That's why dancers practice the same routine repeatedly, often breaking it down into separate actions. But be warned that the "memory" involved isn't necessarily of the *right* way to perform an action. Instead, it's a memory of the *usual* way you have performed an action (whether you did it right or not). Here's one of the simplest—and most surprising— experiments in the entire book, and it demonstrates the scientific principle of muscle memory in super-quick time.

THE LINEUP

★ A doorway

★ You

PLAY BALL!

 Stand with your hands by your sides, palms facing inward, in an open doorway.

 Keeping your arms straight, push out with each arm so that the back of each hand is touching the door frame.

 Press against the frame as hard as you can with each hand.

4 Keep up this pressure for 30 seconds. If you don't have a watch, count "one Mississippi, two Mississippi . . ."

TWO-MINUTE WARNING You might find it easier to use a narrow door frame because it's less tiring to hold your arms lower down for 30 seconds.

5 Step out of the doorway and shake your arms a bit.

6 Move each arm just a little bit upward—they'll both continue to rise up without any prompting from you!

SLO-MO REPLAY ▷

Doing something continuously, as you've done at the start of this simple experiment, involves sending out messages repeatedly from your brain to your muscles. It's a concentrated version of doing the same activity regularly over a longer period. The brain sends the instructions to the muscles using the pathways of neurons (nerve cells). And the official medical term for this "learning through repetition" is neuromuscular facilitation. That's a mouthful! "Facilitation" is just a fancy-schmancy way of saying "making it easier."

Did you notice something else? It wasn't just easier to lift your arms, it was almost impossible *not* to lift them. You can now see how bad habits (poor dance steps, the wrong pitching delivery, chewing with your mouth open) are so hard to break. That's one reason why coaching is so important: A coach checks on your technique before you teach your muscles with repetition.

HOW DO YOU
STOP A CUE BALL
IN ITS TRACKS?

IT'S YOU (THE "COLORADO COUGAR") AGAINST your cousin ("Milwaukee Mike") in the final round of the Summer Camp Eight Ball Challenge. Sweet victory is yours if you can put away the eight ball sitting 15 inches straight out from a side pocket. No problemo! Only . . . if you line it up straight and pocket the eight ball, you'll lose, because the cue ball will probably follow it right into the pocket for a scratch. Or will it? Didn't you read somewhere (wasn't it *Wildly Spectacular Sports Science*?) that

you can hit another ball full-on and your cue ball can stop in its tracks? Hmm, it was something about elastic collisions and that English scientist named Newton . . .

COLLISION COURSE

Momentum (the combination of an object's mass and its movement) explains what goes on in lots of sports. In this case, we're talking about what happens to both momentum and kinetic (movement) energy when two billiard balls collide. If you tap the cue ball just *below* its equator (the middle of the ball), it will skid rather than roll toward the eight ball. When they collide, the momentum and kinetic energy transfers to the eight ball, and the cue ball stops. It's a great example of an elastic collision—the type where one or both objects move after they hit because the momentum and energy have been conserved. If you strike the cue ball *above* the equator, it will roll (rather than skid) toward the eight ball, and some of that rolling-forward spin causes the cue ball to continue. Of course, the ideal way to demonstrate all this is to try it out yourself on a pool or billiards table. But if you're nowhere near one of those (and don't feel much like sneaking into a noisy biker bar), you can test the principle with all types of other sporting collisions.

THE LINEUP

★ 3 golf balls

★ Clear space on a carpeted floor

PLAY BALL!

 Line up two golf balls so that they touch.

 Put the third ball down on the floor about 15 inches from either ball (but positioned so that the three form a line).

15"

TWO-MINUTE WARNING

Remember that these are golf balls, so they're lively! Don't overdo the speed, or you might create a real collision with something breakable in the house. Try doing the experiment several times, working up the speed a little each time.

3 Roll the ball firmly but accurately along that imaginary line toward the nearer ball.

4 "Your" ball—and the ball it hit—should stop dead and the third ball should roll off.

SLO-MO REPLAY ▶▶

You've taken the cue ball example up a level by adding a third ball, but the experiment still relies on conservation of momentum. The momentum of the first ball transferred to the second, and then on to the third—the one that wound up moving.

You can see the exact same effect in a common "desk toy," called Newton's Cradle. (This dude Newton is everywhere!) Five touching metal balls are suspended from a frame using thin wires. When you pull away one of the outer balls and let go, it swings back and hits the others. The three nearest balls stay still but the far ball swings away . . . and then swings back and does the same thing in reverse. The three central balls never move, but the outer ones do. Why doesn't it go on forever? Well, some of the energy is transferred to friction and noise, so the kinetic energy is a little less each time.

CHAPTER FOUR

Winter SPORTS

 Would a downhill skier, pulled over for speeding on the highway, have the nerve to face a stern state trooper and say, "I was just checking out the drag while I was in the egg"? And have you heard the one about the cross-country skier who was heading uphill when—wait, *uphill*? Come again?

Eggs, uphill skiing, even walking on snow. Jeez, things sure get a little crazy when the thermometer drops below 32°F! Maybe it's the cold air making us a little loopy, but winter sports do have their share of weirdness.

But weirdness is a bit like magic. Things start to look different if you look closely. And science is there to help you look *really* closely at what lies behind all winter sports. It could be hockey players using the boards as a teammate, or a figure skater spinning so fast that she's just a blur, or a ski jumper setting off into the wild blue yonder. The one thing that links all of them together is science. And you're going to feel pretty cool figuring out these winter wonders.

PLAYING THE BOARDS?

THE 42-INCH-HIGH BOARDS SURROUNDING
an ice rink are key to the exhilaratingly fast pace of a hockey game. Unlike other sports, such as football, soccer, or basketball, where play often stops when the ball goes out of bounds, the boards keep the puck in play and the action going. Those boards often shudder as players check one another and collide into them, and they're usually marked with dozens of black smudges where pucks have hit at high speed. Sometimes the boards are even

called a "sixth teammate," because players learn to ricochet the puck off them, either to clear the puck in dangerous situations or to pass to a teammate when opponents are closing in.

BRIGHT-ANGLE TRIANGLE

Don't worry, you don't need to go down to the skating rink and "suit up" with all that bulky (and probably very stinky) equipment to understand how hockey players can "play the boards." It's easy to do in a darkened room, with two friends and a flashlight. One of your friends will be your "teammate" on a power play in the dying seconds of the game when you desperately need the tying goal. You've got to pass the puck to her (or in this case, tag her with your flashlight beam) while your other friend is defending. He's doing his best to block that beam of light heading to your teammate. He's crowding you out big-time, and the precious seconds are counting down. If only you had someone else to pass to . . . or maybe some*thing*. It's worth a try!

THE LINEUP

★ 2 friends

★ Powerful flashlight

★ Darkened room

★ Wall-mounted (or dresser) mirror

PLAY BALL!

 1. Choose one of your friends to be your teammate and the other to be your opponent.

 2. Ask your teammate to stand in one corner of the room while you stand (with the flashlight) diagonally across the room at the far corner. The mirror should be on one of the long walls between the two of you.

 3. Your other friend (the opponent) should stand between you, but much closer to you.

 4. Explain that you've got to complete a pass to your teammate by shining the light on her, and that your other friend is to try to stop you.

TWO-MINUTE WARNING You can play your roles pretty seriously—maybe even timing the game with a watch alarm to "end the period"—but be sensible and don't let any of the three of you go near the mirror in the dark. You want to learn something about hockey and geometry, but you don't want to wind up with seven years of bad luck in the process.

5 Start playing. Your opponent should be blocking your "passes" by taking the beam of light.

6 Turn the beam away from your teammate and aim at the mirror. You should be able to bounce the beam off the mirror and onto her—and avoid the oppponent.

SLO-MO REPLAY ▶

You've just used some very nifty geometry to get past the opponent. The light reflects off the mirror in the same way that a puck bounces off the boards in a hockey rink. The angle that formed when the beam hit the mirror (or when a puck hits the boards) is called the angle of incidence. Math theory—and basic instinct—tells us that the angle of incidence is identical to the angle of reflection (where the light leaves the mirror or the puck bounces off the boards). People playing pool or billiards use the very same technique when they "play the cushions," trying to avoid one or more balls by bouncing the cue ball off the sidewalls of the table.

Sport	**HOCKEY**	TIME FACTOR · · · · *10-15 minutes*

WHY ARE HOCKEY STICKS CURVED?

CHECK OUT PHOTOS OR FILM CLIPS OF THE NHL in the 1940s and 1950s, and you'll see that hockey's had a few changes over the years. Yes, that's right—the goalies aren't wearing any masks (not recommended), but we're

looking at something else: sticks. For decades, players used straight sticks without even the slightest curve. Then take a look at photos or clips from the late 1960s. Along with wild hair and crazy mustaches, you'll see some amazing sticks, with curves so big they start to look like fishhooks. Eventually the NHL created rules to limit the amount that sticks could curve, but even today just about every stick has some curve—even goalie sticks. What's it all about?

GETTING AROUND

Until the mid-1960s, the NHL's leading scorers usually notched between 30 and 50 goals per season. But with the introduction of curved sticks, the leading totals jumped to between 60 and 80. The curve adds control to the slap shot, which had become popular in the 1950s. It also adds more control to the wrist shot, in which the puck rolls off the stick with the flick of a player's wrist. The curve even gives the puck more spin, which in turn increases its role as a gyroscope (but more on that later). You can see how this gyroscopic motion stabilizes the spinning puck in the following experiment. Stability and control translate into better shooting—and way more goals.

THE LINEUP

★ Front wheel of a bicycle (20-inch)

★ Safety gloves (2 pairs)

★ Pliers (2 pairs)

★ Friend to help you

PLAY BALL!

1 Make sure you have about an inch of the threaded bike axle jutting out on both sides of the wheel.

2 Wearing safety gloves, use a pair of pliers to grasp one of the protruding axles.

3 Keep the pliers holding the axle and grasp the other end of the axle with the second set of pliers.

4 It's more comfortable starting the experiment with the wheel vertical, so hold it upright while still clamping the pliers tightly.

GYROSCOPE

TWO-MINUTE WARNING

The gloves are important so that you won't get your fingers jammed in the spokes. Your friend should wear a pair also, because spinning the wheel over and over can get painful. Do this experiment outside!

 5 With the wheel held firmly in front of you, have your friend give it a spin.

6 Your friend should continue spinning the wheel so that it increases speed.

7 Take a step back and try to turn the wheel so that it's horizontal. It will resist, so try turning it in other directions—left or right.

8 It should be very difficult to change the wheel's direction from its vertical starting point.

SLO-MO REPLAY ▷

Once it started spinning, the wheel began to behave like a gyroscope— a device that uses the property of angular momentum to stay spinning in the same place. Gyroscopes are a good way to begin thinking about how curved sticks affect a hockey shot. The curve gets the puck spinning while it's still "on" the stick, and the spinning increases as it rolls along the stick's inside curve. Once airborne, the puck holds its position (just like the spinning bike wheel).

So the spinning puck, which started off level on the ice, stays parallel to the ice as it travels through the air. Staying in this position means that its narrow edge presents the smallest possible surface area as it flies. That narrowness reduces drag, the air friction that slows things down. So the puck stays on course at the fastest possible speed.

Just What HAPPENS WHEN WE SKATE?

IT'S AN EXCITING SENSATION WHEN YOU LACE up your skates for the first time each winter. Once you've "found your feet" on the ice, nothing feels better than that gentle push with your leg to send you gracefully forward. Or perhaps your first outing comes complete with stick, pads, and helmet—and you're racing down the ice

on a breathtaking breakaway. But just what is it about the ice that lets us slide and speed along its surface? The key is a thin layer of water on the surface of the ice. It's the water that's slippery, not the ice beneath it. And what causes the ice to melt and create this lubricating layer? It's usually below freezing when we skate!

BRRR . . . ICE UNDER PRESSURE

This experiment is ideal for exploring some of the science tied in with skating. After all, it's really about something thin and metal pressing down on the surface of the ice. The pressure of the wire as it's pulled down by the weight of the bottles is just like the pressure of your skate as you push off while skating. As you'll see, what the pressure does to the ice—and what happens when "the pressure's off"—is the key to it all.

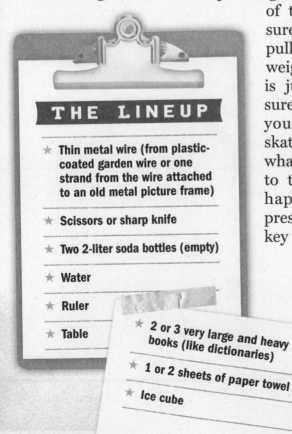

THE LINEUP

★ Thin metal wire (from plastic-coated garden wire or one strand from the wire attached to an old metal picture frame)

★ Scissors or sharp knife

★ Two 2-liter soda bottles (empty)

★ Water

★ Ruler

★ Table

★ 2 or 3 very large and heavy books (like dictionaries)

★ 1 or 2 sheets of paper towel

★ Ice cube

PLAY BALL!

 Cut a piece of wire about 18 inches long. (You'll need an adult to strip the plastic coating off if you're using garden wire.)

 Fill both bottles with water and screw on the caps.

 Loop one end of the wire around the neck of one bottle and tie it tightly.

 Do the same with the other end of wire and the other bottle.

5 Lay the ruler on the table so that it juts out slightly (about 2 inches).

6 Pile the heavy books on the rest of the ruler, so that it's held in place securely.

7 Cut a piece of paper towel in half, then fold it over on itself about four times until it's roughly the size of the jutting ruler.

TWO-MINUTE WARNING Make sure you have enough room for the bottles to hang without touching the floor. And as stated above, only adults should cut or strip wires.

8 Lay the folded paper towel on the ruler and then place the ice cube on it.

9 Pick up both bottles and lower them evenly on either side of the ice cube so that the wire connecting them crosses midway along the ice cube.

10 Slowly lower the bottles so that they're hanging still. The pressure of the wire melts the ice and the wire sinks through it.

11 Wait about 30 seconds and pick up the ice cube. It's whole again!

SLO-MO REPLAY ▶

Everyone agrees that when we skate—or fall—on ice it's because we've actually slid across water. It's a bit like waterskiing. But scientists disagree how and why the ice melts to produce this water. Some say that it's heat from the friction of the skate rubbing against the solid ice. But as this experiment shows, pressure can cause melting as well. The wire wasn't exactly sawing its way through the ice (creating friction and heat to melt it)—it was simply pressing down, thanks to those big bottles.

So the pressure of the wire (or skate) melts some ice, which makes it slippery and easier to skate on. But how can you explain the fact that once the wire had "pressure-melted" its way through, the ice froze up and became whole again? Once the wire was removed, the ice's low temperature was cold enough to restore itself.

How Do Figure Skaters Spin SO FAST?

IN OLYMPIC WOMEN'S FIGURE SKATING, THE free skating program is a dazzling four-minute display of speed, balance, and technical skill, all with the grace

of ballet dancers. The skater will perform a bewildering sequence of twists and turns, but most of the crowd's *oohs* and *aahs* are reserved for the spins. Oftentimes, after a spectacular run of jumps and loops, the skater will then spin, spiraling in with tighter and tighter circles. Eventually she'll stop moving forward or backward, only whirling faster and faster on the spot. How did she get from graceful sweep to spinning top so quickly and effortlessly?

LET'S TWIST AGAIN

The answer is surprisingly simple, even if learning how to do it on the ice takes years of practice. You can test—and demonstrate—the science behind the spin literally without leaving your chair. It's all about angular momentum, or the amount of motion of a rotating object. Just make sure you have enough room to give yourself (or be given) a good spin without bumping into anything else. It works best on a carpeted rather than hardwood floor.

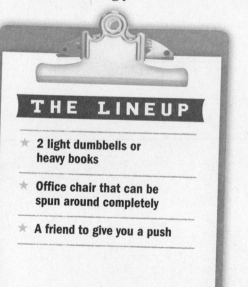

THE LINEUP

* 2 light dumbbells or heavy books

* Office chair that can be spun around completely

* A friend to give you a push

PLAY BALL!

 Hold a dumbbell or book in each hand and sit down on the chair.

 Hold each arm outstretched to make sure you have enough room to spin around freely.

 Keeping your arms extended, kick along the floor to get yourself spinning. It's easier, though, to have a friend start you spinning.

 Once you've reached a good (but still safe) spinning speed, pull the dumbbells or books close to your chest.

 You should notice that you speed up as they get closer to your body.

 **TWO-MINUTE WARNING** This is a safe experiment, but it's worth double-checking that the wheels at the bottom of the chair are locked. You're demonstrating spin and angular momentum here, not the force of collisions between your chair and the rest of the furniture!

SLO-MO REPLAY ▷

You've just demonstrated how angular momentum works. The dumbbells (or books) gained momentum when you applied that initial force by kicking off the floor or getting a push. If you let go of them right away, they'd go straight off, thanks to that momentum. But because you were holding them, their motion became circular. As you pulled your arms in— just like a figure skater—you made the weights' circular path smaller.

But remember that they still had the same momentum, so they covered that smaller distance faster. (You've probably seen the same thing when something in a sink goes around faster and faster as it gets closer to the drain.) As the weights spin faster, they start to pull you around faster and faster, too. Maybe next time you could try this demo on the ice or at a roller-skating rink—but leave the dumbbells at home!

WHY DON'T ALL SKI JUMPERS? CRASH?

EVER THOUGHT OF CLIPPING ON A PAIR OF SKIS without poles and racing down a steep, snowy ramp that will launch you 500 feet through the air? Sounds exciting, huh? Well, crazy as it may seem, ski jumpers do it all the time, and they call on science to do two opposite things with each daring jump.

First, they tuck themselves into a streamlined shape to *reduce* drag (friction from the air) as they shoot down the ramp to build up speed. Second, after takeoff, they spread themselves out to *increase* drag to provide the loft for more air time . . . and to slow their fall when they land.

WANNA LIFT?

This is an easy two-for-the-price-of-one experiment that explains how ski jumpers stay airborne and then land safely. The first experiment is an awesome way of understanding the "angle of attack"—the angle between oncoming wind and a flat object moving through it, like an airplane wing (or ski jumper). That helps determine lift (the force pushing up on an object), one of the basic principles of flight. The second experiment deals with another feature of flight: drag. That's the friction that air itself causes, which slows the forward movement of flying objects. But it's also what lets ski jumpers slow down just enough to land safely. It took humans many thousands of years to understand drag and lift enough to build the first airplanes—you can learn about it in five seconds.

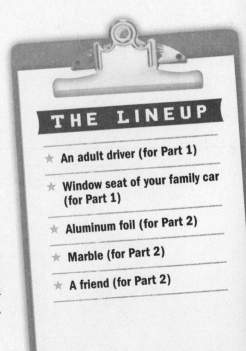

THE LINEUP

★ An adult driver (for Part 1)

★ Window seat of your family car (for Part 1)

★ Aluminum foil (for Part 2)

★ Marble (for Part 2)

★ A friend (for Part 2)

PLAY BALL!

PART 1

 1 Make sure you explain to the driver what you plan to do; agree on a safe time and place when the car won't be going too fast.

 2 Roll down the window all the way.

 3 Hold your hand flat, with fingers and thumb tightly together.

 4 Reach out of the window, palm facing down, and bend your elbow to a right angle (with your palm still parallel to the road).

 5 Hold your arm still and move your wrist so that your fingers begin to point upward.

6 You should feel the air pushing your whole hand and arm upward.

TWO-MINUTE WARNING

Make absolutely sure that you ask permission to perform Part 1. A surprise movement by the window can sometimes distract another driver on the road or block their view. Also, you'll agree on the best time for you to do it: The car doesn't need to be going fast for it to work. And under no circumstances should you perform this experiment out of the window of an F-16 Fighting Falcon jet aircraft, either.

PART 2

 1 Tear a piece of foil so that you have roughly a square shape.

 2 Hold the foil level and ask your friend to hold the marble—they should be level (both at arm's length).

 3 Count to three and then drop both at the same time.

4 Scrunch up the foil into a tight ball and repeat Steps 2 and 3.

SLO-MO REPLAY ▷

You just tested angles of attack in Part 1. Notice how the wind can send your hand up? Newton's second law shows that the angle sends oncoming air downward, and "for every action there is an opposite and equal reaction." That's what pushes your hand (and that winter athlete) up. Ski jumpers do the same thing—they build up speed as they race down the ramp but switch to a different position to catch the wind as they launch. Once airborne, they stretch out straight and lean over their skis, which are in a V shape, in an angle of attack to catch even more lift. The steeper the angle, the more lift they get. They want enough to keep them aloft, but not too much to slow them down.

Drag also acts as a brake. In Part 2 you saw how the sheet of foil's extra space receives the air and slows it right down. When the same foil (an object of the same mass) is scrunched up, it travels more quickly. Ski jumpers are "scrunched up" to maintain speed on the ramp and "opened out" as they control their landing.

What DO SKIERS MEAN BY "THE EGG"?

WHAT DO YOU SUPPOSE IS ON A SKIER'S MIND as he hits 90 mph on a World Cup downhill course? "Am I nearly there yet?" "Did I just miss a gate?" "Is the next turn sharp left or right?" "Who would win in an epic battle: a zombie or ninja?" He knows the answers to all of those—well, maybe not the zombie one—either instinctively or by studying the ski course carefully beforehand. The answer will stagger most people who value their safety. It's "How can I go *faster*?" Whether it's the World Cup or Winter Olympics, speed is the name of the game. The difference between first and second place often comes down to just hundredths of a second, so skiers use specific body positions to go faster. And since 1960, that position has been "the Egg." Yummy!

GOING DOWNHILL...
FAST?

The main challenge for men's and women's downhill competitors is to build and maintain speed. And like racing cars, airplanes, bike racers, and even marathon runners, they face a big obstacle: air resistance. This resistance, called drag, is a form of friction. And one way to lessen that friction—and go faster—is to cut through the air with a narrow profile. (Just think of a rocket, with its needlelike nose cone.) In the late 1950s, French downhill skier Jean Vuarnet developed a streamlined position known as "the Egg." He bent forward so that his head was lower than his back, with his elbows tucked close to his body. In other words, he presented a "small target" to the onrushing air as he skied. That has been the standard downhill position ever since. The following experiment will show you why.

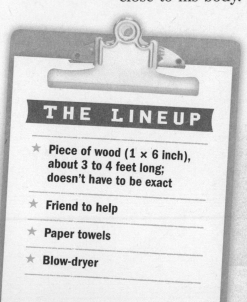

THE LINEUP

★ Piece of wood (1 × 6 inch), about 3 to 4 feet long; doesn't have to be exact

★ Friend to help

★ Paper towels

★ Blow-dryer

PLAY BALL!

1 Lean the board against a sofa or chair so that it forms about a 30-degree angle (one third of a right angle). You don't have to be exact because you'll be testing different slopes.

2 Ask your friend to roll up the paper towel loosely, to form a ball about the size of an orange.

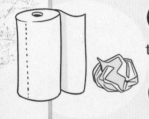

3 Place the blow-dryer at the base of the slope, pointing up.

TWO-MINUTE WARNING Make sure that adults in the house give you permission to use both the blow-dryer and your choice of experiment site.

Have your friend position the paper ball at the top, uphill from the blow-dryer.

 Turn the blow-dryer on to the lowest setting and have your friend let go of the paper ball. Note how long it took to reach the base.

 Ask your friend to roll up the ball more tightly, forming a ball about the size of a golf ball.

 Repeat Steps 3 to 5.

Try arranging the board to form different-angled slopes and test more paper towel balls—a new ball at each slope to make the comparisons accurate.

SLO-MO REPLAY ▶

Whether a skier is standing upright or tucked into a neat egg, her mass is the same, but her speed can vary greatly depending on body position. Staying too upright on a turn can lose a split second and cost her a medal, so it's important that she stay "in her egg" for as long as possible in a run. This experiment is a small-scale but accurate representation of the effects of streamlining. The paper towel has the exact same mass in each of its "runs," but scrunching it up tightly (into a paper egg) really gives it the edge.

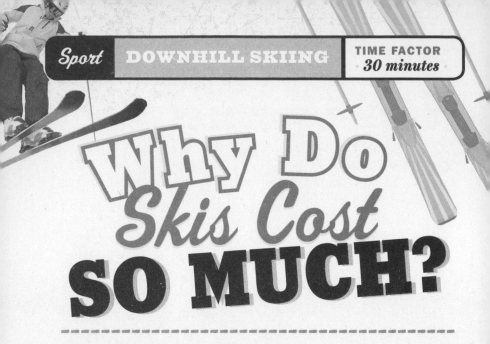

Why Do *Skis Cost* SO MUCH?

YOUR PARENTS HAVE DECIDED THAT THIS IS finally the winter that the whole family learns to ski. So Dad heads off to the sporting-goods store to buy some brand-new skis. He returns looking pale, eventually spluttering, "I think I might need to get a second job if we're going to take up this sport. I had no idea . . ." As he heads off again in search of rentals, you start investigating the science of skis—he doesn't mind spending if there's a scientific explanation! But just what is it?

CORE QUALITIES

Like any good lasagna, it's all about layers. Engineers constantly test new materials and technologies to make each layer stronger, lighter, and more flexible. The ideal ski is flexible along its length to allow schussing (making a fast, straight run down through the snow) and also firm width-wise so that it can keep control on icy patches. Overall, the different layers provide both advantages— not to mention a hefty pricetag.

The outer layers (bearing the logo) are the top sheet— a thin, protective layer of fiberglass, nylon, wood, or mixtures of them all—and the base, made of polyethylene plastic to protect the inside. The next layers in, known as composite layers, have two jobs: to provide strength against twisting and to protect the core of the ski. They "sandwich" the core, one above and one below. Fiberglass is the main ingredient, but sometimes extra layers of other materials (carbon fiber, titanium, or Kevlar) are added to provide different advantages. Finally, at the core of each ski is . . . that's right, the core. That's where things haven't changed so much over the years. It's made of long strips of good old wood, laminated for strength. It may not be fancy, but that's where the flexibility comes from. And this experiment will show you how strips of wood also have a whole lot of strength.

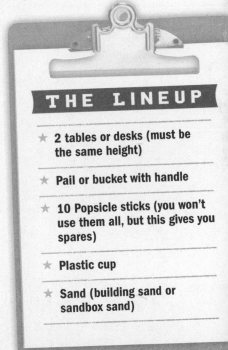

THE LINEUP

★ 2 tables or desks (must be the same height)

★ Pail or bucket with handle

★ 10 Popsicle sticks (you won't use them all, but this gives you spares)

★ Plastic cup

★ Sand (building sand or sandbox sand)

PLAY BALL!

 Push the tables or desks together until they're about 2 inches apart.

 Lift up the pail so that its handle emerges from the gap between the desks.

 Feed a Popsicle stick under the handle of the pail.

④ Lower the pail so that it hangs from the Popsicle stick; adjust the stick and the desks so that ½ inch of stick rests on each desk.

 Slowly add a cup of sand to the pail and observe what happens to the stick.

TWO-MINUTE WARNING

Pails, sand, and breaking sticks can spell trouble if you're doing this experiment anywhere near delicate objects. It's best to perform it outside, or else somewhere that's easy to sweep clean.

⑥ Continue adding sand, cup by cup, observing the stick until it breaks. Note how many cups it took to break it.

⑦ Dump the sand into its original container and repeat Steps 2 to 6, but with two sticks arranged side by side. Compare the number of cups.

⑧ Dump the sand again and repeat Steps 2 to 6, this time with one stick on top of the other.

CAN YOU REALLY SKI UP A MOUNTAIN?

CROSS-COUNTRY SKIING MAY NOT GIVE YOU the butterflies-in-your-stomach feeling of a death-defying double-diamond downhill run. But when you lace up the boots, step into your skis, and set off from your own back door, you can see why the sport is so popular—and so awesome. In fact, one of the great advantages of cross-country skiing—apart from the sense of freedom

as you explore forest trails—is that you can actually ski *uphill*. That's right: uphill. What type of skiing can defy gravity? It defies science! Or does it?

WHAT GOES UP . . .

Cross-country skis are versatile—they're designed to go downhill, along level ground, and even uphill. The trick is in the curved shape, which you can see best side-on. If you lay a ski on the ground with the binding up, you'll see that the middle portion—where your foot slips into the binding—is on the high point of the curve, and the very front and very back are the only bits that touch the ground. When you're ski-ing downhill, your weight is forward and not pressing down on the middle very much. The curve of the ski stays in place and the sticky wax or fabric beneath the boot binding stays above the snow. When skiing across level ground, you press down with one foot in each stride (and the ski flattens to give you traction) while you slide the other foot forward (with the sticky bit off the snow). Skiing uphill is similar, except that you press down even harder, gaining even more traction with each stride. You'll see exactly how with your very own miniature cross-country skis in this experiment.

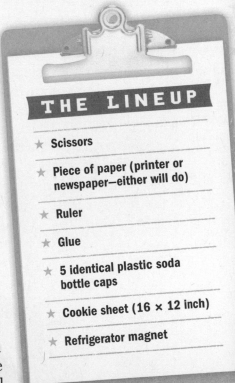

THE LINEUP

★ Scissors

★ Piece of paper (printer or newspaper—either will do)

★ Ruler

★ Glue

★ 5 identical plastic soda bottle caps

★ Cookie sheet (16 × 12 inch)

★ Refrigerator magnet

PLAY BALL!

 Cut 2 strips of paper (8 × 3 inches).

 Carefully apply glue on the rim of all 5 bottle caps.

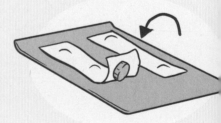

③ Press a cap (rim side down) onto each end of one piece of paper, midway along the 3 inches.

④ Do the same with the second strip of paper.

 Glue the remaining cap as close as possible to the center of the first strip; it should have 3 caps more or less in a line.

⑥ Place the strip with 3 caps lengthwise down on the cookie sheet with one end almost touching the narrow side of the sheet.

TWO-MINUTE WARNING If Step 10 doesn't work, check your cookie sheet and replace it with one that does attract the magnet.

7 Place the other strip down on the sheet about 6 inches from the first. Gently pull it taut so it extends to the same length as the first.

8 Carefully lift the end of the cookie sheet near the two strips; continue lifting until both slide down the sheet.

9 Replace the two strips in their original positions and rest the refrigerator magnet midway down the strip that has 2 caps.

10 Repeat Step 8; the first strip will slide down as before, but the second will be anchored by the magnet.

SLO-MO REPLAY ▶

The sliding of the strips in this experiment corresponds to the sliding of cross-country skis. The third cap, in the middle of the first strip, acts like the built-in arch in a cross-country ski—lifting your foot so that it doesn't press too hard into the snow and "bite." The second strip shows what happens when your foot does press down (as you make your way uphill).

The "stickiness" of the magnet is like the weight of your foot, "grabbing" the snow so that you can push off (and up) again. You put a lot of pressure on each foot in turn as you ski (more like stride) uphill. That's when the skis flatten out so that the special sticky wax, or the high-friction material, on the underside of the ski touches the snow.

CAN YOU REALLY WALK ACROSS DEEP SNOW?

FRENCH TRADERS TRAVELED TO CANADA IN the early 1500s with one thing in mind: furs. North America had what seemed to be an unlimited supply, but those fur traders faced a big problem—Canada is covered in deep snow for months on end. The French were stuck

until the North American First Peoples showed them how to make snowshoes, which they'd been using for thousands of years. Crafted from bent wood and intricate crisscross lacing, these shoes distributed a person's weight as he walked across the surface of the snow. The French called them *raquettes* because they resembled early tennis rackets. Snowshoes are still essential winter footwear for reaching remote settlements in the winter. Over the years, people also began using them recreationally, to explore snowy wilderness areas. Whether by instinct, trial and error, or observing how animals traveled across snow, early snowshoe designers understood the science of how they work.

GET MY DRIFT?

The ancient inhabitants of North America weren't the only people to develop snowshoes thousands of years ago. Early examples have been found in Scandinavia, Central Europe, and northern Asia. While the North Americans continued to develop larger and more effective shoes for walking across the snow, most of these other people turned to ways of gliding across it—by inventing skis. The "tennis racket" style of traditional Canadian snowshoes still works like a charm, but why? Let's take a look with this experiment.

THE LINEUP

★ Bedsheet

★ 8 pillows

★ Chair (dining room style)

★ A friend to help

★ Ruler or tape measure

★ 2 tennis rackets

PLAY BALL!

 1 Spread the bedsheet on the floor and make two piles of four pillows; the piles should be side by side.

 2 Place the chair next to the two piles of pillows.

 3 Have your friend take off her shoes and step up onto the chair.

 4 Ask her to step off carefully onto the two piles of pillows— one foot on each.

TWO-MINUTE WARNING The sheet is there to stop the pillows from touching the floor directly. Try to make sure they don't. And you don't want to be using your dad's expensive new tennis rackets—"the older the better" is the motto for this experiment.

Wait for her to settle and measure the distance from the floor up to her heels.

 Your friend should step down and help you plump up the pillows.

 Set the pillows and chair up as in Steps 1 and 2 again.

 Put a tennis racket on top of each pile and repeat Steps 4 and 5.

SLO-MO REPLAY ▶▶

It won't be hard for you to work out that the tennis rackets represent the *raquettes* that those early French traders observed in Canada and the pillows represent the soft snow. Without snowshoes (when your friend went in with just socks), a person sinks in because their body weight is concentrated on two feet—a relatively small area. The snowshoes (or tennis rackets), however, spread that weight over a much wider surface area. That means that more snow holds a person up and redistributes their weight, so they don't sink in nearly so far. Here's an example to make you think: The heel of a high-heel shoe sinks deeper into sand than an elephant's footprint. Same principle—minus the snow.

How Do SNOWBOARDERS DO THOSE FLIPS?

SNOWBOARDING IS ONE OF THE MOST EXCIT-ing crowd-pullers at the Winter Olympics. Boarders race through slalom courses, dodge obstacles, and perform hair-raising tricks after flying off jumps. They're also in an outdoor classroom, performing a physics demonstration. That's right: Every single twist, spin, and flip calls

for combinations of all those science terms you might have thought existed only on blackboards or in textbooks—words like momentum, velocity, center of mass, and acceleration. (It's a long way from the grungy idea of snowboarding that some adults still have!) The key to some of those jaw-dropping tricks is being able to harness a special force called torque. It's all about getting the most from those rotations and spins.

TIME TO TORQUE

One of the most dramatic snowboarding tricks is the flip. The boarder comes straight down to a jump, gaining linear (straight-line) momentum. The "trick," of course, is to turn that linear momentum into angular (rotational) momentum. And that's where torque comes in. Simply put, torque is a force that causes rotation. Turning a wrench to loosen a bolt is a form of torque. So is turning a doorknob, or pushing the door open so that it swings on its hinges. In each case, the object has an axis of rotation. The snowboarder in mid-flip is spinning around his very own axis of rotation, and his job in the moments before the jump is to increase that spin. This experiment is a great way to take torque from the pages of a science textbook and put it somewhere far more familiar to you—the playground. You'll see that you've been solving torque problems all along, even if you didn't realize it!

THE LINEUP

★ A partner—someone heavier than you (like an older brother, sister, or parent)

★ Playground seesaw

★ You

PLAY BALL!

1. Ask your partner to sit on the seesaw well in front of the normal seat, about 2 feet from the center.

2. Your end of the seesaw will be pushed up, so climb onto it from the center.

3. Position yourself exactly as far away as your partner (about 2 feet from the center).

4. Your end will still be pushed up, so wiggle and slide back slowly.

TWO-MINUTE WARNING It's hard to think of anything dangerous with this experiment, apart from the normal precautions that you'd take at a playground.

Eventually you'll reach a point where you're balanced.

 Go a little bit farther back, and you will descend and your partner's side will go up.

SLO-MO REPLAY ▶

What you've done in slow motion is exactly what the snowboarder does a moment before taking off for the flip maneuver. It's a basic feature of torque. After all, you didn't gradually become heavier as you moved back, so there must be another reason why you eventually balanced the seesaw.

This goes back to some basic science: Lengthening a lever gives it more force—and more torque. That's why a long wrench works better than your fingers when loosening a nut. As you wiggled back, you created a longer lever at your end of the seesaw, eventually giving you enough torque to lift your partner's side. The physics term for that type of lever is the "moment arm," or the distance from the axis of rotation. A snowboarder approaches a jump in a crouching position. He increases his moment arm by straightening his legs just as he takes off. It's as if you slid back on the seesaw really suddenly. That move gives him a burst of torque to power him through those daring flips.

WHY DO Snowboards NEED WAXING?

ANYONE WHO'S BEEN AROUND SNOWBOARDERS knows that they spend a lot of time either scraping wax off their boards or putting it back on. But the bottom of a snowboard is pretty smooth already, so why all the wax? It's all about reducing friction, right? Let's look at some of the jobs that wax can do, and then get a hands-on chance to see how well it does one of those jobs.

LETTING THINGS SLIDE

The big enemy of smooth gliding when you're snow-boarding (or skiing) is friction, the resistance that an object experiences as it moves over another. A snow-board can slow down from different types of friction:

DRY FRICTION: Snow crystals (which are pretty jag-ged—think of a snowflake) will rub against the base of the snowboard, which isn't as smooth as you think. Waxing helps by forming a barrier to smooth out the uneven surface of the base.

WET FRICTION: When melting snow is soft and contains lots of water, it collects in tiny grooves in the base and tries to stick to other water in the snow. (Maybe you have seen something similar if you've tried to separate two panes of wet glass.) Snowboarders use a wax containing water repellant to reduce wet friction.

ELECTROSTATIC FRICTION: This is a bit harder to picture, but the base running across the snow can produce a static-electric charge, which is a bit like the charge that causes socks to stick together when they come out of a dryer. A special wax with an antistatic ingredient is just what the doctor ordered.

THE LINEUP

★ Piece of wood
   (about 1 × 6 inches)
   about 3 feet long

★ Candle (or ski wax,
   if available)

★ Table

★ Ice cube

★ Pencil

Still not confused? How about this: Some wax helps by actually *creating* friction! That is, at least just enough to melt ice and snow to create a slippery surface, exactly like what happens when you skate. This experiment is

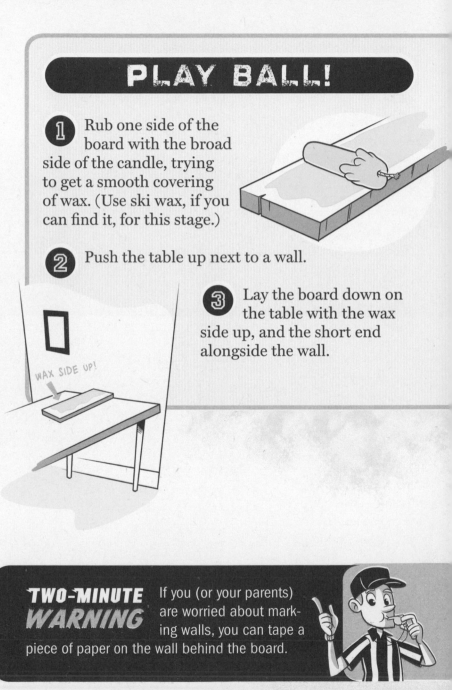

PLAY BALL!

1 Rub one side of the board with the broad side of the candle, trying to get a smooth covering of wax. (Use ski wax, if you can find it, for this stage.)

2 Push the table up next to a wall.

3 Lay the board down on the table with the wax side up, and the short end alongside the wall.

WAX SIDE UP!

TWO-MINUTE WARNING If you (or your parents) are worried about marking walls, you can tape a piece of paper on the wall behind the board.

a quick way of seeing how wax helps deal with dry friction—except you'll turn things on their head. Instead of seeing how an object glides across ice, you're going to try to get ice to glide across an object (the board).

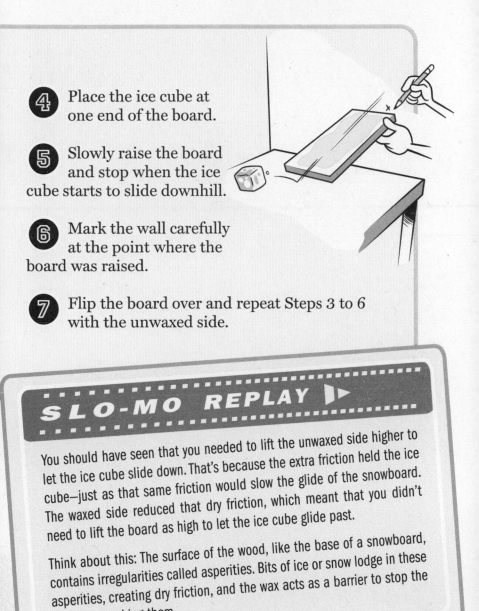

4 Place the ice cube at one end of the board.

5 Slowly raise the board and stop when the ice cube starts to slide downhill.

6 Mark the wall carefully at the point where the board was raised.

7 Flip the board over and repeat Steps 3 to 6 with the unwaxed side.

SLO-MO REPLAY ▶

You should have seen that you needed to lift the unwaxed side higher to let the ice cube slide down. That's because the extra friction held the ice cube—just as that same friction would slow the glide of the snowboard. The waxed side reduced that dry friction, which meant that you didn't need to lift the board as high to let the ice cube glide past.

Think about this: The surface of the wood, like the base of a snowboard, contains irregularities called asperities. Bits of ice or snow lodge in these asperities, creating dry friction, and the wax acts as a barrier to stop the ice from reaching them.

CHAPTER FIVE

On the MOVE OUTSIDE

he very first sports event was probably a footrace. Runners from different parts of what is now Greece competed in the original Olympic Games nearly 2,800 years ago, and we can assume that people had been holding races long before that.

Human beings have been on the move for as long as anyone can remember. What those ancient Greeks would have made of hang gliding or auto racing is anyone's guess. But pretty soon they'd understand that these sports were part of the same yearning to go higher, faster, and farther. And that's exactly what athletes continue to strive for at every level. Whether it's kids in the schoolyard, sprinters lining up for the 100m final, or pole vaulters looking for that extra inch, they're harnessing science to get their best performance.

In this next section, you'll have a chance to understand more about how these sports combine skill, science, and sometimes a large dash of technology to help athletes break records, win races, or just have fun. Are you ready to roll? Let's go!

How Do GEARS HELP YOU GO UPHILL?

"SO I'M THINKING IT'S ABOUT 44:11 FOR THAT big hill up ahead."

"No way! It's too steep, it's gotta be 22:34."

Who do you suppose is having that conversation—two computers? A couple of math professors on their coffee break? Nope, it's two cyclists, discussing the best way to ride up a steep hill. And those funny numbers (gear ratios, really) have to do with which gears they use to make that climb. Apart from being in shape and having cheetah-like strength in your legs, the most important way to climb steep hills on your bike is to find the right gear ratio. Scientists classify gears as "simple machines"—tools to increase force and reduce your workload. You'll soon see how.

CHAIN REACTIONS

Most modern bikes, especially mountain bikes, have lots of gears. Take a look at those circles of teeth (usually three of them) by the base of your bike pedals up front. The chain slots onto one of those three circles (called "chain rings") and also onto one of the seven or eight toothed circles (called "cogs") by the back wheel. The relationship between the chain ring and the cog determines how easy it is to pedal and how far you go with each turn of the pedals. If a turn sends you a long distance, then you need to work pretty hard. But it takes less effort to propel you a shorter distance, which is especially useful for riding uphill.

Those numbers at the beginning refer to which gear a cyclist chooses: It's the number of teeth on the chain ring followed by the number on the cog. A big first number (like 44) shows that you're pulling lots of the chain around. But a small second number (like 11) shows that the chain is on the cog that uses fewer teeth to move the wheel around. Still sounds a bit too mathematical? Time to get a bike out and check it out for yourself.

THE LINEUP

★ Grown-up to help

★ Bicycle with 21 or 24 gears (most mountain bikes have this many)

★ Chalk

PLAY BALL!

① Have your grown-up helper hold the bike up off the ground while you change the gear to the lowest number on the left gear (1), guiding the chain ring, and the lowest on the right (1), for the cog in back.

② Let your helper rest by putting the bike down. Make a chalk mark on the back tire.

③ Raise the bike again and note where the chalk mark is, then slowly make a full revolution of the pedals; note how much of a full circle the rear wheel makes (by checking the mark).

TWO-MINUTE WARNING

Bike-repair shops have special clamps to hold bikes off the ground; you probably don't have one of those, so that's why you've called on a grown-up to be your own personal Arnold Schwarzenegger and do the heavy lifting. And remember: You should always be pedaling when you change gears, and that goes for this experiment, too.

4 While the bike is still being held, change the gears to the highest numbers for both the chain ring and cog. (Don't worry if your bike only "changes gear" on the cog—you can still do the experiment.)

5 Let your helper rest again for 30 seconds or so.

6 Repeat Step 3 and note how many circles the wheel makes (once more using the chalk mark as a guide).

SLO-MO REPLAY ▶

A ratio is simply a comparison of quantities with the same unit. A bike's gear ratio (those weird numbers at the beginning) compares the teeth on the chain ring up front and the cog on the rear wheel. If the first number (how many links you've pushed) is small, it means you don't have to work as hard to do a full pedal stroke. You're halfway toward making it easier to climb. You now want that second number to be *larger*! That's so those same links that you've just moved don't have to move in as much of a circle. That single pedal stroke was easier on your legs but wouldn't get you as far.

Think of that ratio like a fraction: chain ring teeth divided by cog teeth. A lower ratio (like 14:44) is "easier" to pedal than a higher ratio (like 42:12). Still a little puzzled? Think of a lower gear ratio as taking baby steps and a higher one as big strides. It takes more baby steps—but a lot more pedaling—to climb a hill.

Does a HEAVIER CYCLIST ROLL DOWNHILL FASTER?

YOUR UNCLE FRANK HAS BEEN BRAGGING all Thanksgiving Day about how good a cyclist he was at your age, and that even now, 20 years after his last race, he could still beat you. Okay, enough talk—the race is on!

Half an hour later, you're about 300 yards from the top of dreaded Hangman's Hill. You gave your uncle a two-minute head start because he'd "put on a few pounds lately," but you're closing in on him. Sure enough, you catch him right at the top, and now it's time for the three miles home, all downhill. You've done the hard bit—nothing could go wrong now, could it?

MASSIVE VICTORY?

You're not just confident in your bike skills—you think science is on your side, too. Uncle Frank's definitely tired, so he'll probably just freewheel downhill all the way home. And gravity (the reason you can freewheel) creates the same acceleration as it pulls things, no matter what their mass is. So even though you're less massive than your uncle (now *that's* an understatement), you'll be pulled down at the same rate and keep your slight lead all the way. Only, your confident uncle thinks that he has science on *his* side, for a slightly different reason. Time to investigate.

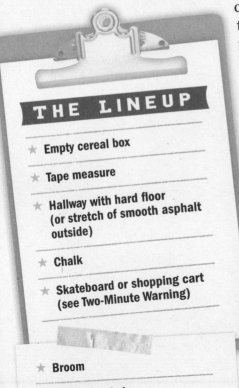

THE LINEUP

★ Empty cereal box

★ Tape measure

★ Hallway with hard floor
(or stretch of smooth asphalt outside)

★ Chalk

★ Skateboard or shopping cart
(see Two-Minute Warning)

★ Broom

★ A friend to help

★ Large dictionary
(or 2 large phone books)

PLAY BALL!

 Set the cereal box upright near the end of a hall, leaving about 8 feet clear behind it.

 Make a chalk mark on the floor (or the ground) by the front edge of the cereal box.

 Make another mark 10 feet in front of the first chalk mark.

 Take the skateboard to the other end of the hall.

 Stand behind the skateboard with the broom resting on it, ready to push it forward.

TWO-MINUTE WARNING Make sure you have enough room to do this experiment properly if you decide to do it inside. If space is tight (you probably need about 45 feet), then do it outside. If you can't get hold of a skateboard, ask the manager of your local supermarket whether you could do this experiment in the parking lot with a shopping cart—with adult supervision, and when it's not busy. Finally, that marching rhythm isn't just for entertainment: It's to ensure that you apply a consistent force, so make sure you keep to it.

 Agree on a marching rhythm (like "ONE-two-three-four, ONE-two-three-four") with your friend, so you'll push the skateboard in time to that beat.

 Begin "marching" to that beat and push the skateboard down the hall to the second mark you made.

 Pull the broom away when you reach the mark. This may be a bit tricky.

 The skateboard will knock the box over and then continue. Measure from the "cereal box mark" to the front of the skateboard (where it stopped).

 Set the box back up and take the skateboard back to the other end of the hall, adding the dictionary (or phone books).

 Repeat Steps 7 to 9.

SLO-MO REPLAY ▶

The answer to "Who's right about winning this race?" is . . . both of you, in a way. Your experiment's second "roll"—with its extra mass, just like Uncle Frank—went farther. It's true that gravity *does* produce the same acceleration on everything, regardless of its mass. (NASA astronauts demonstrated that on the moon, when they dropped a feather and a hammer: They landed at the same time.)

But that pesky uncle of yours points out that we're not on the moon—we have air resistance on Earth to slow us down, and we need force to overcome it and let us go faster. Sir Isaac Newton proved that force = mass × acceleration, and you have the same acceleration, because of gravity. But Uncle Frank's mass is much greater, which means that the force that he produces (to fight air resistance) will also be greater. *Grrrrr.* Don't you hate it when grown-ups are right?

WHAT HAPPENS WHEN SKATEBOARDERS PUMP?

SKATEBOARDS HAVE COME A LONG WAY since kids with corduroys and flannel shirts rolled noisily down sidewalks in the 1950s. Today's skaters mix daring moves like 1080s (three complete midair spins) and McTwists (spin-twist combinations) along with old favorites like the Ollie and the Kickflip. As a result, a skateboard display can look like a cool mash-up of gymnastics, surfing, and street-smart heroics. Oh, and also like a science class. Some skaters might not look like your typical physicist—at least in action

$E=MC^2$

at the local half-pipe—but they're certainly packing in a lot of scientific principles with each move.

PUMP IT UP!

Let's look at a showstopping trick, like the 1080, to discover exactly where the science comes in. The main ingredient is height—you need to get some serious air, with enough room and hang time to spin three times. And for height you need speed in the takeoff. That's why skaters use a curved riding surface, like a half-pipe, to build up angular momentum (the momentum of spinning or rotating). The skater crouches down on the approach to the curved side, and then pumps—standing higher on the skateboard. The result: a burst of speed to take him into the jump. You've done the same thing every time you've pumped a playground swing to go higher. Your legs are extended on the downswing, then pulled right in as you head up again. Check out this easy experiment to see what you were doing—and how skaters use the exact same scientific technique.

THE LINEUP

★ Balloon

★ Water

★ Scissors

★ String

★ Ballpoint pen tube (the plastic shell surrounding the ink tube)

PLAY BALL!

 1 Blow up the balloon, then let the air out.

 2 Add enough water so that the balloon doubles in size and then tie it off.

3 Cut a piece of string about twice as long as your arm.

 4 Tie one end of the string around the balloon knot so that the balloon will hang down when you pick up the string.

5 Feed the other end of the string through the pen tube and hold on to that end of the string in one hand and the tube in the other.

TWO-MINUTE WARNING Do we need to tell you that this one's a "better do it outside" experiment? Well, we just did anyway!

Hold the tube up at arm's length and pull on the string so that the balloon hangs down.

 Move your hand holding the tube in a circle so that you get the balloon swinging in a circle.

8 Continue swinging the balloon until you reach a steady speed.

9 Without stopping the swinging, pull the string hard with your other hand—the balloon will speed up as the string gets "shorter."

PULL ARM!

SLO-MO REPLAY ▷

Imagine the curve of the half-pipe as being part of a full circle. Each roll—either up or down—taps into the power of angular momentum. And the distance between a center of mass and the center of that circle dictates how fast an object (like a balloon here, or a skater) moves around. The closer to the center, the faster the spinning movement. In the pump right before a trick, the skater stands up higher and moves her center of mass closer to the center of that imaginary circle. It's very similar to pulling the string so that the center of mass (the balloon) moves closer to the center (your hand holding the pen tube).

How Do Long Jumpers "Walk" In Midair?

THE SPECTACULARLY SPEEDY LONG JUMPER begins her run, gaining velocity as she approaches the board. After about 20 strides, she hits top speed, plants a foot, and launches herself into the air—she's airborne! Newcomers to this Olympic sport will expect her to fly feet-first in order to land with outstretched legs and gain the most distance. But that's when something odd happens: Midway through her jump, when she's just about at the highest point, she begins to "walk." Her feet are nowhere near the ground! Does that make sense, or is it a great big waste of effort? Well, world record–holders (both women and men) have been using this technique for decades, so *something* must be working!

SWIMMING LONG JUMP?

To get the most explosive launch, the long jumper pushes off with her legs and leads with her body. But to get the best distance, she needs to land with her feet well in front of her body. So what happens in between? And where does this "walking" come into it? Imagine sprinting down a track and then stopping short abruptly. The top of your body would start to lunge forward. That's exactly what happens when the long jumper stops the run and takes off. Her body is rotating across her center of mass with angular (rotational) momentum. The walking motion in midair, called the hitch kick, helps to reverse that motion. As she approaches her landing, she throws her arms upward and then shoots them down quickly. That helps swing her legs forward so that she can land feet-first, and her linear (straight-line) momentum will carry the rest of her body past her feet. You can get exactly the same effect next time you go for a swim—right about now!

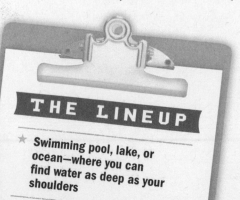

THE LINEUP

★ Swimming pool, lake, or ocean—where you can find water as deep as your shoulders

PLAY BALL!

 Stand where the water is up to your shoulders and swim around for a minute or two so that you're accustomed to the depth.

 Make sure there's no one very close to you.

3 Swim along the surface of the water mainly kicking, with your arms as close to your sides as you can manage.

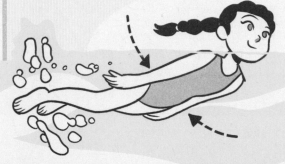

TWO-MINUTE WARNING Never take risks while swimming. Make sure that you have others with you and that you're in an approved swimming area with lifeguards. And try not to eat too many jumbo-sized chili dogs before swimming, either.

Keeping your arms by your sides, try to stop and stand up.

5 Return to normal swimming, with your arms in front of you.

6 Repeat Step 3 but bring your arms quickly down in front of you—your legs should swing forward just as quickly, letting you stand up.

The move you made in Steps 5 and 6 is almost identical to the long jumper's move near the end of the jump. Like you, she had her arms extended above her (out in front of you, in this experiment). Then she swung them down quickly to let her legs swing forward to the ideal landing position. All this swimming and air-walking business depends on angular momentum, which is a bit of a confusing term, because it usually deals with things rotating and not at straight angles. But like all momentum, it's conserved: The momentum can be transferred but never destroyed. Your legs shot forward to "conserve"—or in this case, balance—the momentum of swinging your arms down.

Why Are Pole Vaulting Poles So Bendy?

TO THE NON-DAREDEVILS AMONG US, POLE vaulting is one of those daunting activities that ranks up there with cliff diving and free-fall parachuting. We wring our hands and wonder: Can't they find a stronger pole? That one bends so much! But it turns out that the pole is bendy *and* strong—an ideal combination for something that transfers energy during a collision. If that sounds even more worrying, keep on reading. You'll

see how pole vaulters harness science to keep them safe while going for altitude records.

A SWINGIN' GOOD TIME

A pole vault is a great example of conservation of energy, which tells us that energy can't be created or destroyed, just transferred. The pole vaulter begins with lots of potential energy (from things like the Wheaties she ate that morning and her natural muscle strength). As she makes her approach and gains speed, she converts that energy into kinetic (moving) energy. But to lift off the ground, that energy also needs to be transferred from horizontal to vertical energy, and that's where the pole comes in. The more it bends, the more potential energy it stores to help with the launch. Thanks to Newton's third law (every action has an opposite and equal reaction), it straightens out and converts that potential energy into vertical kinetic energy, and the athlete springs upward. Here's an experiment that you can do at your local playground, as long as you can find a grown-up brave enough to believe in conservation of energy. They should!

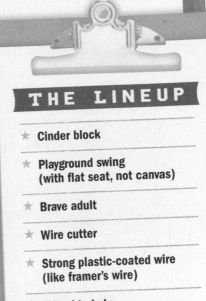

THE LINEUP

- ★ Cinder block

- ★ Playground swing (with flat seat, not canvas)

- ★ Brave adult

- ★ Wire cutter

- ★ Strong plastic-coated wire (like framer's wire)

- ★ Friend to help

- ★ 1 length of wood (any thickness) 6–7 feet long

PLAY BALL!

 Carefully put the cinder block on the swing.

 With the adult's help (including the wire cutting), secure the block to the swing using three lengths of wire.

 With you and your friend each holding one side of the swing, draw it back until it is about 5 feet off the ground.

 Ask the adult to stand right behind the swing, with his nose almost touching it.

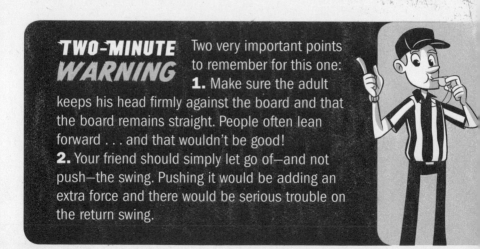

TWO-MINUTE WARNING

Two very important points to remember for this one:
1. Make sure the adult keeps his head firmly against the board and that the board remains straight. People often lean forward . . . and that wouldn't be good!
2. Your friend should simply let go of—and not push—the swing. Pushing it would be adding an extra force and there would be serious trouble on the return swing.

 Adjust the swing and the adult's position in case there's any slack in the swing; the chains should be very tight.

6 Ask your friend to continue holding the swing in place while you stand the wood upright so that it touches the back of the adult's head.

 Tell the adult to stand completely still, with his head always touching the wood, until the experiment is finished.

8 Ask your friend to let go of the swing—without pushing it at all—so that it swings forward.

9 It will swing back and almost touch the adult, but not quite.

SLO-MO REPLAY ▶

This experiment might not seem too similar to pole vaulting, but it really depends on the same principle of conservation of energy. The swing built up lots of potential energy as you drew it back and up. When you released it, the energy transferred to kinetic energy as it swung forward, just like a pole vaulter. The total amount of energy (potential plus kinetic) remained the same—it only changed form. As the block climbed on the other side, the kinetic energy began storing again as potential energy. Once it had all been transferred, the "pendulum" (swing) started to come back again. But wait! With all that transfer of energy, why didn't the swing come back all the way? Some of the energy was transferred to heat energy through friction and even sound, so there wasn't quite the same amount of kinetic energy on the return flight.

WHY DO DISCUS THROWERS Spin Around First?

THE HISTORY OF THE DISCUS GOES WAAAAAY back to the original Olympic Games thousands of years ago in ancient Greece. Very few of us today have ever held a discus, but we generally seem to know what to do with it: Throw it! But how? When we throw most things—footballs, baseballs, and even javelins, another field event—it's mainly done

in a linear (straight-line) way. You make a short running start and chuck it forward. But discus throwers don't go about their business in anything like a straight line. In fact, they go around and around in a small space before sending it off for a long throw. How can all that spinning motion translate into a straight throw?

DISCUSSING THE DISCUS

A discus thrower translates his strength into kinetic (movement) energy as he spins around one and a half times. Meanwhile, centripetal force—the force drawing the discus toward the thrower's body—also builds up. Centripetal force pulls objects directly toward the center of their circular motion, which in this case is the thrower himself. When he lets go, the centripetal force stops and the angular (spinning) velocity becomes linear (straight line). The discus flies off in a direction that's a 90-degree turn from the radius (the imaginary line from the center of the discus to its spinning edge). In other words, it goes flying straight off after spinning.

Here's a chance to get a much smaller disk moving with centripetal force. Maybe you'll eventually work your way up to the discus.

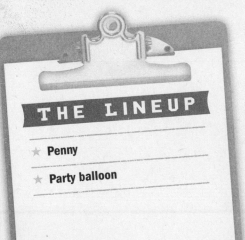

THE LINEUP

★ Penny

★ Party balloon

PLAY BALL!

1. Slip the penny into the deflated balloon. Hold the balloon by the neck to make sure that the coin has fallen into the wider part of it.

2. Blow up the balloon and tie it shut (with the coin inside).

3. Hold the balloon with the knot under your palm and your fingers extending down and around it.

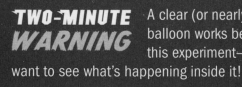

TWO-MINUTE WARNING A clear (or nearly clear) balloon works best with this experiment—you want to see what's happening inside it!

Turn the balloon upside down so that the knotted end under your palm is pointing up.

 Move your hand in a circular path so that the coin begins to spin around inside the balloon. You might need to try this a few times if the coin seems to bounce around.

6 Eventually you'll get the coin to spin around smoothly.

SLO-MO REPLAY ▶

The wall of the balloon supplied the centripetal force to keep the coin spinning. The discus thrower's arm does the same job, pulling the discus toward him. If the balloon suddenly popped, the coin would stop spinning and fly off in a straight line, just as the discus does.

WHY CAN'T YOU SPRINT FOR A WHOLE Marathon?

LEGEND HAS IT THAT IN 490 BC, A SOLDIER named Pheidippides ran nearly 25 miles to tell the people of Athens about their dramatic success at the Battle of Marathon. Exhausted, he arrived to deliver a simple message, *nike* ("victory"), then collapsed and died. Modern marathons, staged in the Olympics and in cities

around the world, have a slightly longer course: 26 miles, 385 yards. The world record for the marathon is just over two hours, which is an amazing achievement. But what if someone like Usain Bolt, the fastest person ever timed and longtime holder of the 100m record, ran flat-out for a marathon? If he averaged 10 seconds for each 100 meters, he'd run the roughly 42,000 meters in just an hour and 10 minutes. Hey, those marathoners had better watch out for the Lightning Bolt. But things aren't quite so simple.

FEEL THE BURN

Every time a muscle contracts, it burns glucose (a simple sugar that provides energy), which then breaks down into something called lactate. Normally this moves through the blood and the person gets rid of it through the lungs. Just think of how heavily people breathe after exercise. The trouble starts when the muscle is burning up glucose so fast that the body can't get rid of it quickly enough. That's what happens when we "overdo it," and the body has ways of telling us to stop: cramps, stomach pains, and even vomiting. Marathon runners stay right on the safe side of these warning signs for the whole race, averaging amazing five-minute miles—but no one could sprint anywhere near that far or long. You can "feel the burn" briefly (and harmlessly) in the following experiment. It's a good thing you don't have to do it for two hours!

THE LINEUP

★ Clothespin (wooden type with spring)

★ Watch, clock, or phone that can time seconds

PLAY BALL!

 Hold the clothespin with your arm outstretched; it doesn't matter which hand.

 Count how many times you can squeeze the clothespin in 60 seconds.

 Continue counting, and see how many you can do in the next 60 seconds. Stop if it's too hard.

TWO-MINUTE WARNING Don't be afraid to stop this experiment even before the first 60 seconds are up. You'll have proved the scientific principle sooner than expected!

SLO-MO REPLAY ▷

Chances are you "felt the burn" even during the first minute. Your muscles were burning up glucose fast enough for the lactate to begin building up. It's just one of the warning signs that your muscles are working too hard, which would certainly happen to someone trying to sprint a marathon. If you squeezed the clothespin far less quickly, you'd find that you could go on for much longer. That's why marathon runners pace themselves over the course of the race.

CAN THE
Right Shoes
GIVE YOU
THE EDGE?

THE MOST BASIC, NATURAL SPORT IS undoubtedly running, which harks back to prehistoric times when humans chased down—or were chased by—wild animals. It's no wonder, then, that running became one of the first organized sports, going back far beyond the time of the original Olympic Games in ancient Greece. Those early athletes ran barefoot, and later runners wore ordinary walking shoes, but it was only in the 20th century that shoes were designed specifically for running. It's about time!

UNLIKELY COMBINATION?

People run to the store to buy "sports footwear" mainly for two reasons. For one thing, running shoes protect the feet, so that running mile after mile won't cause lasting damage (or a nasty blister). Lots of designs use sweat-absorbing fabrics and formfitting cushioning for increased comfort. The other aim—though harder to prove—is to make people run faster. Some new designs, featuring lightweight materials, claim to increase a runner's speed. After all, you use less energy and feel less tired if you're lifting a lighter load with each step. But shaving time off your race really comes down to the principle of conservation of energy. If more of your kinetic (movement) energy can be saved "for the rebound" with each footfall rather than being absorbed in sound, heat, and vibration, then you'll use less energy and gain some speed. But how to go about getting that "bounce"? Time to experiment.

THE LINEUP

★ Friend to help

★ Yardstick or meter stick

★ Table

★ Chair

★ Tennis ball

★ Water

★ Sponge

PLAY BALL!

 1 Have a friend stand the measuring stick on the table, with numbers reading upward from it.

2 Stand on the chair, holding the ball at the top of the measuring stick.

3 Let it drop and note how high up it bounces.

TWO-MINUTE WARNING Make sure not to do this experiment near lights, china, or other breakables. And don't fall off the chair!

Soak the sponge in water and then wring it out so it is slightly damp but not sopping wet.

 Place the damp sponge at the base of the measuring stick and repeat Steps 2 and 3, dropping the ball onto the sponge.

 Optional: Try repeating those steps using different materials at the base—books, a towel, gloves, sand, whatever you choose.

SLO-MO REPLAY ▶

You've just been testing materials to see whether they provide elastic or inelastic collisions. Remember that an elastic collision retains more of the kinetic (movement) energy so that it (or a runner) needs less energy for the next step. On the other hand, an inelastic collision absorbs much of that energy. For a runner, that "softening" of the blow makes it more comfortable.

As you can see, a material normally provides one of those advantages but not the other—it depends on whether the buyer is looking for comfort or to shave seconds off their personal best. But thermoplastic polyurethane (TPU)—a new material in some running shoes—promises to do both. Based on your own evidence, which of your own chosen materials comes closest to combining those qualities?

How Do
Hang Gliders
STAY IN THE AIR?

MAYBE YOU'VE SEEN ONE OF THESE THINGS slowly wheeling across the sky like a vulture or a hawk. At first it looks like a triangular kite, or maybe some sort of parachute—except it seems to be going *up* again. What in the name of Sir Isaac Newton is going on here? Well, it's a hang glider, of course, and the person "holding onto it" is actually guiding it, just like an airplane. It takes a lot of guts just to hang on to one of those engineless aircraft, and it takes even more skill to keep it up there. So how do they do it?

DO I FEEL A DRAFT?

When you talk about anything flying through the air—from paper airplanes to the Space Shuttle—you primarily consider lift and drag. Lift is an upward force that creates flight, and it's the wing's job to provide it. But drag—a force, such as air resistance, that slows the speed—works against it. Aircraft designers often talk about a lift-to-drag ratio, or how much lift and drag a certain wing design produces. They're usually looking to have lots of lift with very little drag. Modern hang gliders score really well because they're so lightweight and can get by without an engine to increase lift. That explains why a hang glider would float pretty much like a paper airplane if you flung it out off a steep hill. But without a pilot, it wouldn't last long in the air. A good pilot can detect air currents that keep the hang glider airborne, and often help it climb. Those helpful currents are called updrafts, and you can create one for yourself in this experiment.

THE LINEUP

- ★ Can opener

- ★ 3 empty, clean metal cans (like soup cans)—10-ounce size

- ★ Masking tape

- ★ 2 paper clips

- ★ Poster putty

- ★ Thumbtack

- ★ 2 books of equal size (old phone books work well)

- ★ Table near a window that receives sunlight

- ★ Ruler

- ★ Pencil

- ★ Piece of ordinary printer paper (cut to a 6 × 6 inch square)

- ★ Scissors

PLAY BALL!

1. Use the can opener to open the top and bottom of each can; throw away the lids.

2. Pile the cans one by one to make a tower, wrapping masking tape completely around each "joint" to secure it.

3. Straighten the paper clips and tape both of them to the inside of the top can's rim so they point up. They should be opposite each other and jutting inside the rim about ½ inch.

4. Carefully bend the free ends of the clips so they meet and form an arch.

5. Secure this arch with a little tape where the clips meet, and place a small (pea-sized) ball of poster putty on top.

6. Carefully press the thumbtack (pointing up) onto the poster putty.

TWO-MINUTE WARNING You can set this experiment up anytime you want, but you really need to conduct it on a sunny day to get the payoff.

Lay the books on the table about 2 inches apart and set the tower over the gap, resting equally on each book.

 Use a ruler to measure and mark a line from each corner of the paper toward the center, stopping ¼ inch from the center in each line. Cut along the lines.

 Now bend every *other* corner of the paper down to the center and tape them in place. You should have a pinwheel shape.

10 Carefully balance the pinwheel (taped side down) on the point of the thumbtack.

11 When exposed to the sun, the pinwheel should start to spin.

SLO-MO REPLAY ▶

A hang glider can work its way through breezes and winds just like a kite, but to stay aloft for long periods it needs to find updrafts. These channels of rising air are usually tied to warmth—for example, the warmed air rising up from rocks that have been baking in the sun. You've created an updraft in this experiment. The sunshine warms the air inside the tower, causing it to rise up and spin the pinwheel. And it constantly sucks in new air (to be warmed) because of the gap you left at the bottom. Air rushes in to fill the vacuum (empty space) left by the departed air.

Could Bungee Jumpers Go Up and Down FOREVER?

FOR THOUSANDS OF YEARS PEOPLE HAVE tried (and failed) to produce a "perpetual motion machine," a device that, once set in motion, can go on and on perpetually (forever). Some designs relied on

the flow of water, while others used magnets to keep things moving. Even Leonardo da Vinci got in on the act, designing an off-center wheel with ball bearings to keep it turning. Close study or practical testing showed that none of these designs would work, because some force would eventually stop them. But what if they were all too complicated? Perhaps a popular new pastime, bungee jumping, might solve this age-old puzzle. After all, don't those jumpers keep on going until someone stops them?

THE EGG BUNGEE

Here's a chance to combine the excitement (and suspense) of bungee jumping with some investigations into perpetual motion. In case you haven't come across this thrilling extreme sport, bungee jumping involves leaping from a great height while connected to an elastic cord. The jumper falls to the end of the cord, which stretches until the person's head almost touches the ground. The cord then yanks the jumper up again, just in the nick of time. You're going to have a chance to make your own bungee jump, with a very brave egg as your test jumper. It might not be off the Golden Gate Bridge or into the Grand Canyon, but the exact same scientific forces will be at work.

THE LINEUP

★ Egg

★ Zip-top sandwich bag

★ Rubber bands (lots)

★ Yardstick or meter stick

★ Poster putty

★ Piece of paper

★ Pencil or pen

PLAY BALL!

1 Put the egg in the sandwich bag and zip it shut.

2 Tie a corner of the sandwich bag to a rubber band in a double knot. (It helps to twist the corner of the bag, pinch the rubber band, and imagine that they're shoelaces.)

3 Place the measuring stick flat against a wall, with one end touching the floor and the "0" end at the top.

4 Secure the stick to the wall with poster putty.

5 Hold the "bungee bag egg" with one hand and the end of the rubber band with the other and let the egg drop. Start your drop at the level of the "0" on the yardstick.

6 Note the lowest point that it reached; you might need to do the drop several times—averaging the distances—to get an accurate reading.

7 Lengthen the bungee cord by slipping two more bands to the end; use the easy slipknot technique.

8 Measure the drop again, once more using an average of several drops.

9 Repeat Steps 7 and 8, getting lower and lower until you are either as far as you can go (without breaking the egg) or feel that the cord can't manage any more rubber bands.

10 When you have stopped adding bands, drop the egg and let it rise and fall until it comes to rest (unbroken, you hope).

TWO-MINUTE WARNING

Be cautious as you work your way closer to the floor in this experiment. Check the distances at each stage heading down. Do the gaps get bigger? Stay the same? Base your judgment about calling it quits or adding another band on this evidence. Oh—and don't use the last egg in the house (in case you miscalculate).

The bungee jump is a great demonstration of the conservation of energy. The jumper (or egg) has lots of gravitational potential energy at the top. It gets converted into kinetic (movement) energy with the fall. Then, as the cord (or string of rubber bands) reaches its limit, it builds up elastic potential energy. And as the cord pulls it back, it gains kinetic energy again for the rebound.

However, as you can see, this process doesn't go on forever. The energy didn't disappear, it just transferred into other forms of energy, like heat (from friction), little wriggles in the cord, and noise (if you heard any faint twangs). So if you wanted perpetual motion, you're out of luck—at least you can make an omelet!

Why Do RACE CARS HAVE *Wings?*

LOW TO THE GROUND, FLANKED BY GIANT wheels, and with only enough room inside for the driver, racing cars look nothing like the family station wagon your mother uses to drop you off at school (unless, of course, Mom happens to be Danica Patrick). A lot of auto racing technology does wind up in passenger cars, such

as high-tech brakes, suspension, and onboard computers, but one feature is particularly striking—the "wings" atop the back trunk. With these cars hurtling around at more than 200 mph, why don't they take off like planes?

FOILED AGAIN!

If you're wondering why the powerful combination of wings and speed doesn't automatically lead to flight, then you're on the right track. You might recall that wings are designed in an airfoil shape, with a curved surface on the top and flatter surface below. Since air passing along the curved surface needs to travel farther (and therefore faster) than the other air, it loses pressure. That's Bernoulli's principle in a nutshell. Well, racing cars have wings in that very same airfoil shape— only they're upside-down! So the side with the stronger pressure is on top, and the car is held on the road more securely. Simple, really. Here's another chance to reacquaint yourself with Bernoulli's principle. Think about how it can work if the airfoil's curved surface is facing up or down.

THE LINEUP

★ Scissors

★ Some lightweight paper (a page from an old magazine works well)

★ Ruler

PLAY BALL!

1 Cut a strip of paper about 10 × 2 inches.

2 Hold the narrow end up to your mouth, pinching each corner with one hand. The paper will be drooping down.

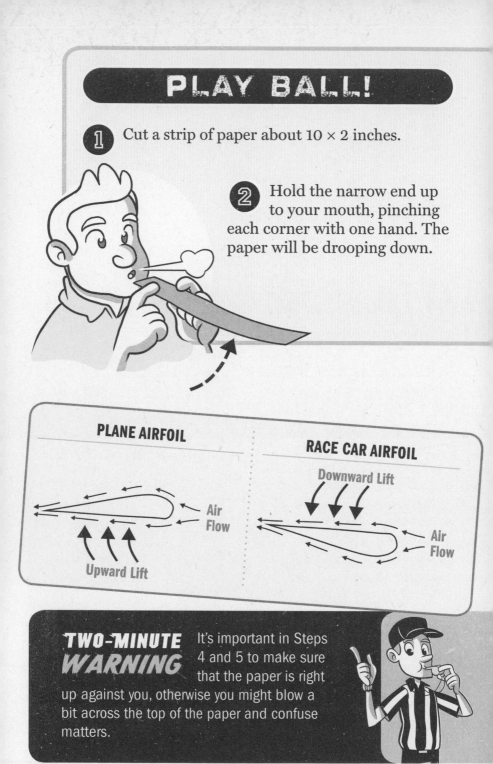

PLANE AIRFOIL

Air Flow

Upward Lift

RACE CAR AIRFOIL

Downward Lift

Air Flow

TWO-MINUTE WARNING

It's important in Steps 4 and 5 to make sure that the paper is right up against you, otherwise you might blow a bit across the top of the paper and confuse matters.

3 Blow steadily across the top of the paper; it should rise.

4 Now raise the paper just a bit so that it touches between your nose and upper lip.

5 Blow again—this time along the bottom of the paper—and the paper will be forced down.

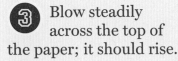

SLO-MO REPLAY ▷

In less than a minute you've shown how an airfoil design can provide lift (the upward force needed for flight) for planes (Step 3) or downward pressure to help high-speed racing cars "hold the road" (Step 5). It's all because Bernoulli's principle demonstrates how fast-moving air traveling across a curved surface loses some of its pressure. And will we ever see these in passenger cars? The answer is yes—we already do. They're normally called spoilers, and you can see them running across the back of many cars. These spoilers aren't there to help the cars travel at 200 mph; instead, they help reduce drag (air resistance) so that the cars can save fuel.

CAN YOU

TIGHTROPE WALK AT HOME?

YOU'VE SEEN PICTURES OF CIRCUS TIGHT- rope walkers making their way across the "Big Top," or maybe other fearless performers crossing the chasm between Manhattan skyscrapers, over a desert canyon, or above Niagara Falls. Yikes. We may think of tightrope walkers as a breed apart, risking their lives in ways we could never dream of doing, but slacklining low to the ground in the back-yard or at the park has become increasingly popular. The "line" is a flat length of netting with adjustable tension to make tricks—as well as normal crossings—possible. Slacklining remains an ideal "do it yourself" sport because people can hook lines up to trees and poles just about anywhere, have a blast, and then pack up and move on.

SLACKERS' SECRET

Though far less dangerous, slacklining still shares a number of features with the death-defying high-wire acts. Most important, the key to any kind of rope walking is being aware of your center of mass—the point in an object (even if that object is you) that's the average of all the mass in that object. In plain English, it's where you can imagine all of the object's mass being concentrated. You can learn a bit more about center of mass in this experiment—but the results might come as a surprise.

THE LINEUP

★ **3 empty fruit juice cartons (59 fluid ounces or similar) with screw-on caps**

★ **Water**

★ **Marker**

★ **Table**

★ **Yardstick or meter stick**

PLAY BALL!

 Fill one carton completely with water and screw the cap back on, marking it "Full."

 Half fill another and screw the cap on, marking it "Half."

 Leave the third empty and screw the cap on, marking it "Empty."

 Line up all three on the table, using the measuring stick to get them straight.

 Predict which of the three is most stable before moving on to Step 6.

 This is one experiment that has its feet on the ground and doesn't call for special warnings or safety advice. Just keep those juice tops screwed on tight.

6 Line up the measuring stick along the back of the three cartons, about an inch down from the top.

7 Push the stick forward very slowly and see which of the cartons will be the first, second, and last to fall.

SLO-MO REPLAY ▷

So is it a surprise that the half-full carton stayed upright? It shouldn't be, because objects with lower centers of mass are generally more stable. The full carton might have seemed like the one that would stand up longest: After all, it has the most mass. But the top half of the half-filled carton is mainly just air, so the center would have to be much lower down.

It's the same with slacklining—or even high-wire acts. Keeping your center of mass lower down and closer to the line (or wire) helps you maintain stability. The trick is to move the line a little from side to side (remember, it's slack, not tight) to keep the base of support under your center of mass. Still not convinced? Stand up straight and ask a friend to shove you over carefully. Then crouch down and ask again. The second try should prove the point about the stability of the lower center of mass.

A Scientific
TUG *OF* WAR?

WHAT DO YOU THINK OF WHEN YOU HEAR THE words "tug of war"? Playgrounds? Summer camp? Muddy clothes? Rope burns? How about "world championships"? Yes, teams of adults compete to be crowned world tug of war champions each year, organized by—you guessed it—the Tug of War International

Federation. Even scientists join in on the fun. No big surprise there—whenever there's mass, velocity, and momentum involved, you'll probably find a scientist studying it. And some of their findings give a clue as to which team will probably win a tug of war.

FORCING A RESULT

At the heart of this experiment is Newton's second law of motion, which examines mass (like weight), force, and movement. The amount of force needed to move an object is proportional (linked mathematically) to its mass. In other words, if someone pushed off against another person who weighed twice as much, the lighter person would go twice as far. (Or the heavier person would go half as far, if you look at it from their point of view.) You've known that instinctively: If you throw a golf ball and a heavy brick with the same force, the golf ball will go farther. You can try some of the same calculations in the following experiment.

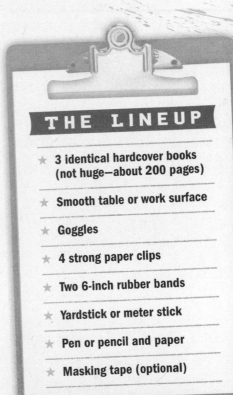

THE LINEUP

★ 3 identical hardcover books (not huge—about 200 pages)

★ Smooth table or work surface

★ Goggles

★ 4 strong paper clips

★ Two 6-inch rubber bands

★ Yardstick or meter stick

★ Pen or pencil and paper

★ Masking tape (optional)

PLAY BALL!

1 Lay two books on the table, about 6 inches apart, with the spines facing each other.

2 Put on the goggles and bend one end of each paper clip into a right angle.

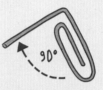

3 Slide the bent ends of each clip into the top and bottom of the spine of each book; the "unbent" end of each clip points outward at the other book.

4 Loop the rubber bands around the unbent ends of the clips so that you have two parallel bands.

5 Slide the books so that the connecting loops are tight.

Put the middle of the measuring stick alongside the gap between the books, so that it extends beyond each book.

 Keeping an eye on the measuring stick, slide each book the same distance away from the other.

 Measure the gap between the books: It should be about 9 or 10 inches.

 Let go and note how far back each book traveled. Then repeat twice so that you have three results. Make an average of these results.

 Place the third book (remember, it should weigh the same as the others so far) on top of one of the two books.

Repeat Steps 8 and 9 three times with this setup, recording and averaging the results.

TWO-MINUTE WARNING

You'll get the best results with three copies of the same book, but otherwise get as close as possible. If you're having a hard time sliding the end of the paper clips into the spines, you can tape those ends to the outside of the binding so that the "unbent" ends of the clips face each other (as in Step 3). And those goggles will protect your eyes from any paper clip shrapnel!

The force you applied (moving books the same distance every time) was identical throughout the experiment. With books of equal mass on each side, the distance back should have been the same. But when you doubled the mass on one side by adding a second book, you should have found that the heavier side moved back only half as far. It's just the same in a tug of war: The team that weighs more overall will probably win. Its combined mass will produce more force (for the same amount of tug) than the lighter team's. That will give it the edge in the "tugging" side of things. And that same mass advantage will make the team harder to be tugged. It's a win-win!

WHAT
Makes a Frisbee
FLY?

FROM KIDS TO COLLEGE STUDENTS TO golden retrievers, just about everybody loves playing with Frisbees. You can play an organized Ultimate game with teams and rules, or just have a lazy toss in the backyard with a pal. But you may have to throw a few passes to a white-coated scientist with wild, frizzy hair, the one over there explaining gyroscopic forces and air pressure. Wait, didn't you see him? Well, either way, he's right. The spinning disk is a great example of gyroscopic force—the tendency of a spinning object to maintain its orientation. That's why a Frisbee stays in a horizontal position throughout most of its flight. But the reason it stays aloft might be pretty familiar by now (since it feeds into so many sports): Bernoulli's principle. Thought you knew everything you needed to know about our buddy Bernoulli? Well, this experiment might add a bit more.

GO WITH THE FLOW

And the winner of the Quickest Experiment to Demonstrate a Complicated Scientific Principle Award, with a time of 2.23 seconds, goes to . . . *drumroll* . . . Go with the Flow! Hey, wait a minute—that's this experiment! Let's check it out.

THE LINEUP

★ Kitchen faucet (the deeper the sink, the better)

PLAY BALL!

1 Turn on the cold water to nearly full blast.

2 Observe the width of the flow near the faucet and also at the bottom.

TWO-MINUTE WARNING

Things would be pretty bad if we had to give any warnings about turning water on and off.

Hold a Frisbee up and look at it sideways. You'll see that the top curves gently up, over, and down, so that the "leading edge" (the rim in front as it passes through the air) is always curved. And the bottom—from rim edge to rim edge—is flat. That's very much the same as the airfoil design of an airplane wing. And that design, of course, allows Bernoulli's principle to kick in. The air passing over the curved top has to move faster (because it has more surface to travel over) and loses pressure, compared to the slower air below, which pushes up and gives the Frisbee its lift.

Back to the faucet: Bernoulli's principle describes what happens to *fluids*, which can mean gases (like air) or liquids (like running water). The water accelerates and loses pressure as it flows down from the faucet. So by the time it hits the sink, the width is much narrower because the air has been able to push in on the faster, "weakened" flow.

CHAPTER SIX

Rackets
and
CLUBS

Now this *really* is where science and sports meet head on. Pick up a golf magazine and you'll find about a dozen articles on how to stand, get the best drives, putt long distances, and keep your nerves steady. You'll find even more pages with ads for products that will do all of those things! "Try this new grip." "Club heads designed for power and distance." "Hole more with this new putter."

And tennis? Surely that's just two rackets and a ball, right? Not so fast. Just look at clips of some classic matches from the 1970s. Try not to giggle at the players' "short-shorts" and instead look at the rackets—they're absolutely tiny. And made from wood! No wonder those rallies still look like patty-cake.

Yes, technology does tie in with these sports in a big way, but there's always the chance to use science to get the best from your own body—regardless of how much you've spent on equipment. You'll soon see how.

How Do You POWER A TENNIS SERVE?

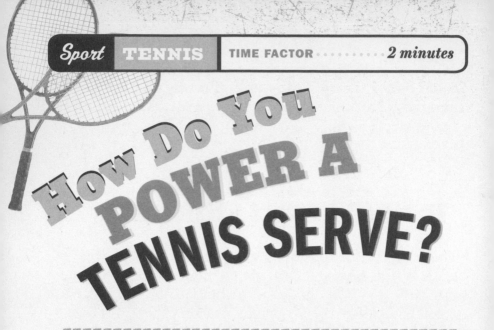

WITH MOST PROFESSIONAL SERVES NOW IN the blistering-fast 120 to 130 mph range, modern tennis is all about the "power game." Decades ago, a top player might hit 10 aces (unreturnable serves) per match, but nowadays that number is often more like 25. So what explains this "power surge"? Well, pro players now have fitness coaches and nutrition experts, and modern rackets help a lot, too: More area on the head (the strung area) and frames made of special materials propel serves in ways people could only dream of in the past. But why do "ordinary" players still feel that their serves are weak, even with the right racket? A simple technique makes all the difference in cranking up the power.

A WAITER'S SERVE?

The problem for most beginners or intermediate players is fear of hitting shots that go out, so we try to play safe with the "Waiter's Serve" technique. (Think of how a waiter holds a tray of drinks over his shoulder, with the tray parallel to the ground—that's the position of a beginner's racket face as she cautiously serves. The racket swats straight down as if it were a flyswatter.) But imagine that, instead of keeping the racket head face-on to the ball all the way through, you hold it side-on as it's behind your head. You still move it forward and down, but only open it (with a flick of the wrist) at the last instant before hitting the ball. That's called "pronation," and it gives a serve its real power.

In scientific terms, pronation is a form of torque, or force that causes rotation. The strange thing about pronation is that most people already do it naturally in other sports and even when they walk (your feet can pronate, too). You'll have a chance to see it in this next experiment, and find out how you can use biomechanics (the study of body movement) to blitz your opponents.

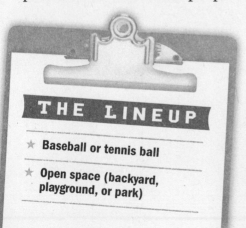

THE LINEUP

★ Baseball or tennis ball

★ Open space (backyard, playground, or park)

PLAY BALL!

1 Hold the ball with your throwing hand as normal.

2 Move your hand so that your palm faces down.

3 Pull your throwing arm straight back so that your hand finishes behind your head—but keep your wrist firm so that the hand doesn't twist.

TWO-MINUTE WARNING Make sure that the only difference between the two throws is in the way you flick (or don't flick) your wrist. It's easy with a "normal throw" to step into it. Clayton Kershaw will forgive you—it's for the sake of science.

Now swing your arm forward (still keeping your wrist firm) and let go exactly where you would in a normal throw.

  Note how far you threw the ball, then pick it up again.

6 This time, throw the ball as you normally would. (To make a fair comparison, don't move your legs in the throw.)

7 Measure the distance of this throw.

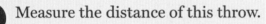

SLO-MO REPLAY ▶

Steps 1 to 4 are the throwing equivalent of the "playing safe" Waiter's Serve: You've done nothing with your wrist during the delivery. Step 6 assumes that you have thrown the ball as you would a baseball, building force with an outward flick of your wrist (to the right if you're right-handed, leftward if you're a lefty). You didn't realize it, but you've just naturally used the same power serve pronation technique.

You'll see that the second throw goes much farther. Distance in this experiment is the equivalent of speed in a tennis serve. It makes a big difference! That quick wrist-flick gives a sudden boost to racket-head speed, and more speed in the racket head translates to more speed in the serve.

Why Are Tennis Balls FUZZY?

"NEW BALLS, PLEASE."

If you watch a competitive tennis match, you'll hear the umpire make this request every nine games. That's not a long time—sometimes no more than 15 minutes—but the rules of the sport call for it. Why? Well, tennis is one of the few sports where the ball can change its behavior quickly. Unlike squash or racquetball, which use similar but slightly smaller rackets, tennis

relies on a ball that "deteriorates" quickly. And the way that tennis players put crazy spin on the ball makes all the difference. Whether it's a heavy topspin forehand or a backhand slice, the racket strings need to linger for a while as they slide across the surface of the ball. A "bald" tennis ball wouldn't give that traction, but a fuzzy, furry ball will.

PICKUP GAME

Whether it's Serena Williams' all-powerful topspin or Roger Federer's skidding backhand backspin, tennis shots rely on the ability of the strings to grip the ball. Some of that grip comes from the tension (tightness) and the material of the strings, but the biggest contributor is the ball itself. And if the top players are blasting shots back and forth in long rallies—coupled with the friction created each time the ball lands—then it's no surprise that this fuzzy surface would wear off quickly. Still wondering how the surface of a ball could play such an important role? Try this awesome experiment to get a string's-eye view . . . and get a grip on the subject!

THE LINEUP

★ Ice cube

★ 2 plates

★ Chopsticks

★ Flour

PLAY BALL!

1 Put the ice cube on a plate.

2 Use the chopsticks to try to pick it up—it will be almost impossible.

TWO-MINUTE WARNING It shouldn't matter what material the chopsticks are made of, although many pairs are lacquered to have a smooth surface, which is ideal for this experiment.

Pour a layer of flour onto the other plate and roll the ice cube in the flour until it's covered completely.

 Try picking it up now with the chopsticks; it should be much easier.

SLO-MO REPLAY ▶

Think of the ice cube as being a tennis ball without the fuzzy surface and the chopsticks playing the part of the racket strings. Tennis involves far more than using the strings as a trampoline to send the ball away. In order for the strings to "grab" the ball and give it a deceptive spin, there needs to be a fair amount of friction in the collision between ball and racket. The fuzz provides that friction—just as the flour on the ice cube provided the friction so that the chopsticks could grab it.

DO TENNIS SURFACES REALLY MATTER?

HOCKEY IS PLAYED ON ICE, WATER POLO IN A pool, and football on a grassy field, but—get this—you can play tennis on more than 160 types of surfaces. (Way back in the day, the picky, crazy-long official rule book forgot to mention anything about court materials!) In fact, the four major Grand Slam tournaments all feature different surfaces: hard asphalt, clay, grass, and a slightly different hard court. Each of those materials often produces its own type of champion—like Rafael Nadal, "The

King of Clay"—because the court surface determines the style of play. For instance, the material affects the height and speed of the ball as it approaches, giving opponents more (or less) time to prepare a return. But is there a way of measuring whether a court surface is "fast" or "slow"?

CAUSING FRICTION

Scientists analyzing the properties of tennis surfaces speak of two main factors: the coefficient of friction and the coefficient of restitution (a coefficient in this case means simply a measure of something). You know what "friction" is all about, so it isn't surprising that a force that resists motion would be important on a tennis court. The "restitution" is really just a fancy way of describing the bounciness of a surface. Players often talk of a "fast" or "slow" court surface. The fastest courts require the quickest reflexes because lower coefficients of friction and restitution mean the ball bounces less. So which surface is fastest? This experiment looks closely at the friction factor and finds a fun way of measuring it.

THE LINEUP

★ Experienced tennis player

★ Friend to help

★ Smooth asphalt surface (like a parking lot)

★ New tennis ball

★ Stopwatch

★ Tennis racket

★ Astroturf welcome mat

★ Sand (enough to fill a half-gallon container)

★ Pencil and paper

PLAY BALL!

Note: *The more experienced tennis player (either you or your friend) will "perform"; the other will time.*

1 Start on a clear patch of asphalt and have the "player" get used to it by using the racket to bounce the ball on it repeatedly.

2 Begin timing and see how many bounces the player can get in 30 seconds.

TWO-MINUTE WARNING This experiment would be much more accurate, of course, if you could do it on real courts (hard court, grass, and clay) but very, very few people are lucky enough to be able to do that.

Repeat four times and record the highest of the five numbers.

 Now place the mat down on the surface.

 Repeat Steps 2 and 3 to get a figure for "grass."

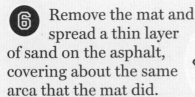 Remove the mat and spread a thin layer of sand on the asphalt, covering about the same arca that the mat did.

 Repeat Steps 2 and 3 to get a figure for "clay."

SLO-MO REPLAY ▶

Even though you probably weren't able to conduct this experiment on the real surfaces, these approximations give you a great idea of how different they are in terms of friction. The surface with the most friction is the one that slowed the bounce down most (leading to the lowest "bounce count").

In real play, the highest-friction surface (clay) slows the ball down most and creates the biggest bounce when it lands, giving the opponent more time to set up shots because it slows momentum. It also leads to longer rallies since it's harder to "put away" shots. Asphalt has a bit less friction, shortening the rallies in each point, but the nearly "friction-free" surface is grass, where the power game is most rewarded. Watch those bounces next time Wimbledon is on, and if the grass gets wet, you're in for quite a treat—that just makes the surface even faster!

What About A RUNNING *Golf Shot?*

JUST ABOUT EVERY GOLF EXPERT AGREES that as you prepare for your drive (the first shot on a hole), you should have everything "just so": feet positioned, upright posture, firm leading elbow, correct grip. Only then can you achieve the balance to transfer your swing into a long-distance drive down the fairway. Is that really true, though? The popular golf comedy *Happy Gilmore* shows a very different—and successful—approach to the game. Happy, the main character, is a hockey player with a mean slap shot. He takes up golf, and instead of steadying himself to drive, puts his hockey skills to good use by charging up and hitting the ball on the run. It's all good for a laugh, but what's actually wrong with the Happy Gilmore approach? Time to experiment, scientists!

SHOW SOME DRIVE

This experiment should be a lot of fun, since you'll test some of the possibilities of Happy's unusual swing. Remember, though, that all of this testing is meant to have parallels with golf, a sport that calls for distance and accuracy. Ideally, you'll find a way to combine both in one go . . . but you'll never know until you "swing" away.

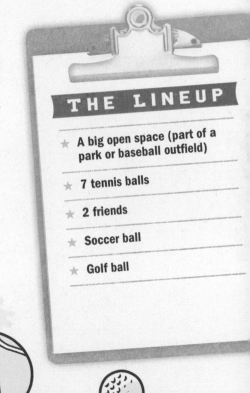

THE LINEUP

★ A big open space (part of a park or baseball outfield)

★ 7 tennis balls

★ 2 friends

★ Soccer ball

★ Golf ball

PLAY BALL!

 Agree on a tee (starting point) and give three tennis balls to each friend.

 Ask one friend to pace 10 steps left from the tee, and the other 10 steps right.

 Your friends should now pace 15 steps forward (keeping the same distance from each other) and each set a tennis ball down there.

TEE! 10' 10' 15' 15' 15'

They should then set another ball down 15 paces ahead of the first, and finally a third ball 15 steps past the second. The balls mark out-of-bounds for the experiment.

 Set the soccer ball at the tee and from a standing start, kick it forward as hard as you can, trying to keep it in bounds.

6 Set the soccer ball at the tee and give it another kick forward. This time, run up to it before kicking.

 Repeat Steps 5 and 6 with a tennis ball and then with a golf ball.

SLO-MO REPLAY ▶

In the movie *Happy Gilmore*, our hero winds up winning a major golf tournament with his approach. You might find something different, though. You probably found that the second (running) shot gave you greater distance—Newton's second law of motion would have predicted that the greater acceleration would produce more force. But what about accuracy? Making contact with a golf ball (either with a club or your foot) calls for precision. All those experts have a point—you'll probably find that the distance you gained with the running kick was outweighed by the lack of accuracy. How many "kick shots" landed out of bounds?

Why Do GOLF BALLS HAVE DIMPLES?

GOLF HAS A PRETTY BASIC SET OF PRINCIPLES to understand: Get the ball into the hole with the fewest shots, do it for 18 holes, and add up the total. The smaller that total, the better. So if you're at the tee (starting point) of a long, 450-yard hole, you want to send that first shot flying as far as possible. No sweat! But something's wrong with your ball—you notice that it's covered in little dents, like dimples, all over.

You reach into the golf bag to swap it for a good one, but that one's covered in dimples, too! Are these joke-shop balls that your brother stuffed into the bag? Nope—you can see that the other players' balls also have those dents all over. What's the deal?

HEY—WAKE UP!

Golf balls didn't always have those dimples. For many years, people played with smooth golf balls. Then players noticed that a ball flew better if it got a little scratched or dented, so they began to add their own dents and bruises. These helped for distance, but the irregular arrangements of the scratches sent the balls flying all over the place. That's when golf ball designers (yes, people do that for a living) created the current "dimples all over" design. They're spaced regularly, as you'll see if you have time to count all 336 dimples on a typical ball (just don't hold your breath if so). Okay, so the nicks, scratches, and dimples do all help. But how? That's where the science comes in, and you'll have a demonstration of your own.

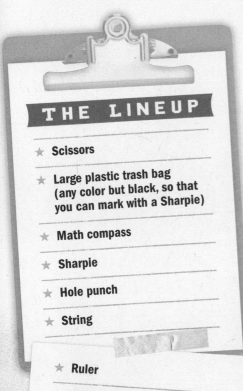

THE LINEUP

★ Scissors

★ Large plastic trash bag (any color but black, so that you can mark with a Sharpie)

★ Math compass

★ Sharpie

★ Hole punch

★ String

★ Ruler

★ Wastebasket or small trash-can lid (about 18-inch diameter)

★ 2 plastic clothespins

PLAY BALL!

 1 Cut the bag down two long sides and across the bottom to make two sheets.

2 Use the compass to draw a 10-inch diameter circle on one piece of plastic.

3 Cut the circle out and punch a hole in the center.

 4 Punch six holes, evenly spaced, just inside the curved edge.

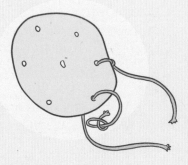

5 Cut six 20-inch lengths of string and tie one end of each to each of the six holes.

6 Place the lid or waste basket down on the second piece of plastic and trace around the edge to make a circle on the plastic.

  This is a safe experiment, but make sure you have an adult to help with the cutting.

7 Repeat Steps 3, 4, and 5 with the second piece.

8 Gather the free ends of the six strings and knot them together, then repeat with the first parachute.

9 Clip a clothespin to the knots you've just made. You now have two parachutes, with clothespin weights.

10 Climb on a chair or ladder and hold a parachute in each hand, keeping them well apart from each other but at the same level.

11 On the count of three, drop them at the same time and note which one wins.

SLO-MO REPLAY ▶

You should find that the smaller parachute lands first, because it left a narrower "wake" behind the moving clothespin. The wider wake from the larger parachute acted to slow things down more. In a similar way, the dimples on a golf ball reduce the wake behind the flying ball. They create a type of turbulence that causes air to stick to the moving ball longer, rather than forming a big V-shaped wake (like the wake behind a moving boat). The smaller wake means that there's less drag—a type of air-resistance friction—to slow down the ball, so it goes farther.

WHAT MAKES the Perfect Putter?

GOLFERS ARE NUTS ABOUT STUDYING THE science of their sport to try to gain an advantage, whether over the course or over other golfers. And just as the engineering advances in racing cars eventually make their way into the family car, lots of golf engineering can apply to other sports. For example, golfers had abandoned wooden-shafted clubs decades before baseball and tennis players started using bats and rackets

PUT
PUT
PUT
PUT
PUT
PUT

made with new materials. One of the most popular elements of golf for tinkering with new designs is putting. Want to see—and demonstrate—some of the simple science that has led to a ginormous development in putters? It might just help you get past that dang windmill on the mini-golf course, too.

IN THE HOLE! (MAYBE)

There's no escaping the fact that a lot of golf success or failure is "in our head." People can use mental tricks to imagine that the hole is bigger (making it easier to putt), or they might get a bad case of "the yips" (like a ticklish feeling in their arms as they swing, which can ruin a shot). But over the years, golf clubs and balls have developed to make shots more predictable and travel farther. This experiment demonstrates just how some basic design principles have made putting that much easier. Forget about the U.S. Women's Open or the Masters in Augusta. What's at stake here is your title at the Krazy Kone Mini-Golf Championships. No pressure!

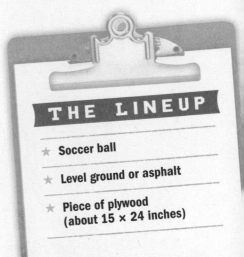

THE LINEUP

★ Soccer ball

★ Level ground or asphalt

★ Piece of plywood
  (about 15 × 24 inches)

PLAY BALL!

 Put the ball on the ground and keep it still.

 Hold the wood along one of the long edges, with one hand midway along the edge.

 Line up the wood behind the ball. (You're pretending the ball is a golf ball and the wood is the putter face.)

4 Pull the wood back like a putting backswing, then swing it forward so that it hits the ball just a little to the left or right of your hand. The wood should shudder a little and twist, and the ball won't roll straight.

TWO-MINUTE WARNING If you can't find a piece of plywood that's the right size (which doesn't have to be exact, anyway), ask an adult to cut a piece from some scrap plywood.

5 Set up the ball again and make another "off-center" putt—but this time hold the wood firmly with one hand above each end. The putter will remain firm, and the ball should roll straight on.

SLO-MO REPLAY ▶

This experiment displayed the key scientific principle in putting: moment of inertia, or "the measure of a body's resistance to angular (rotational) acceleration." For golf club designers, moment of inertia boils down to how much the face of the club (the side that hits the ball) twists on impact. It's this twisting that makes shots go haywire, sending the ball off in the wrong direction.

Old-fashioned "hot dog putters," like the ones you often play with at mini-golf courses, have a low moment of inertia, making it really tough—they are just a single piece of metal with no part heavier than any other. Hitting the ball even a little off-center will twist the putter one way or the other, just like what happened in the first part of this experiment. Modern putters, on the other hand, have a high moment of inertia because they're weighted at both ends (the "heel" and "toe") and not much in the middle, so a ball hitting off-center doesn't cause the putter to twist as much.

CHAPTER SEVEN

Aquatic *Sports*

Here's a chance to make a big splash with your friends as you find out about some of the astounding science flowing through water sports. Have you ever wondered about the four strokes that feature in swimming events? Which is fastest, and why? And is there a right age to take up surfing? Oh, and here's one that has puzzled people (and a few scientists) over the years: How the heck can you sail a boat *against* the wind?

There's a scientific answer to all of those questions, and you'll have a chance to explore the practical spin-offs from learning those answers. You'll want to "dive right in" and test the experiments as soon as you've read these entries.

And speaking of diving, the book ends with a painful experiment: Just what is it that makes belly flops hurt so much? That's the sort of "sports meets science" question that means a lot to most of us . . . and could save us a big pain in the belly once we learn the answer.

Why Are Some SWIMMING STROKES FASTER?

WHEN OLYMPIC SWIMMERS GO FOR A DIP IN those massive 50-meter-long pools, they complete laps in times so fast it'll make your head spin. But if you look closely, you'll see real differences between the lap times in the four main competitive strokes: freestyle (also known as front crawl), butterfly, backstroke, and breaststroke.

That's because each stroke features a unique balance between propulsion (powering forward) and reducing drag (the friction resistance of water). As with lots of other sports, watching the experts' techniques might help us shave off some lap time of our own.

DON'T LOSE YOUR MARBLES

Many factors go into making some strokes faster or slower than others. The rules for each stroke limit swimmers to certain positions and techniques that affect their time. For example, while swimming breaststroke, your arms must stay in the water at all times—which, as you'll see, slows you down. Butterfly limits speed as well by having your chest "plow" through the water like a big old river barge. Here's something else to ponder: The flying fish of the Caribbean, some of the fastest in the world, get a lot of their speed by traveling through the air rather than through water. Could traveling through water really be that much slower? A superquick experiment will help you decide.

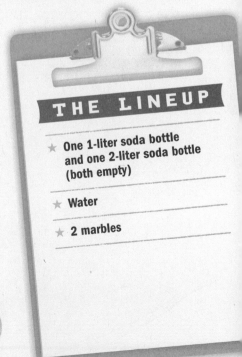

THE LINEUP

★ One 1-liter soda bottle and one 2-liter soda bottle (both empty)

★ Water

★ 2 marbles

PLAY BALL!

 Fill the smaller bottle with water.

 Place it next to the empty bottle.

 Hold a marble over the mouth of each bottle.

 At the count of three, let go of the marbles at the same time.

 Note which marble reaches the bottom first.

Make sure you have the marble resting almost on the water surface before dropping it—a splash would affect the way that it sinks and throw off the results of the experiment.

S L O - M O   R E P L A Y ▶

There you have the proof that water produces much more drag than air. The marble passing through air (the empty bottle, even though it's twice the size) wins easily. So you can see why the breaststroke, which keeps your arms in the water throughout, is the slowest of the main strokes. Your arms need to travel forward against the direction of movement and are slowed by the resistance of the water. The other three racing strokes— freestyle (crawl), butterfly, and backstroke—are all faster because you move your arms back through the air when you've finished your stroke.

HOW CAN YOU *Sail* AGAINST THE WIND?

HAVE YOU EVER WONDERED HOW THOSE ginormously big, fully rigged sailboats actually go where their captains send them? After all, they can't just wait around for the wind to blow them in the right direction. In fact, don't those little Sunfish and Sailfish sailboats at the beach and the lake have the same problem? Sure, it's easy enough to understand how you can sail downwind, with a stiff breeze filling the sails. But how do sailors make their way *against* the wind? Maybe you won't be surprised to learn that there's a scientific answer—and you can test it yourself.

BLOWIN' IN THE WIND

Yes, it's possible to sail against the wind, but not straight into it. No one—not Christopher Columbus, Ferdinand Magellan, or even Captain Jack Sparrow—could manage that. But for thousands of years, sailors have found a way around the problem, even if they didn't think of it in physics terms. The secret to forward motion is "tacking"—making a zigzag course into the wind, so that you're always traveling diagonally. Each zigzag step is called a tack. The wind fills one side of the sail on a starboard (rightward) tack, and then on a port (leftward) tack.

As the wind tries to push the sail out of the way with each tack, that's when Sir Isaac Newton comes on board. Remember "for every action there's an opposite and equal reaction" (Newton's third law of motion)? The wind heading in had to change direction as it bounced off the sail it had just filled. That would have caused the boat to drift sideways. But an underwater, fin-like boat feature, the keel, provides the "opposite reaction" to that redirected wind. Those two forces cancel each other out and the remaining force pushes the boat forward. You can see that first redirection (wind bouncing off the sail) in a simpler way, with the following experiment.

THE LINEUP

★ Magazine

★ Smooth table

★ Ping-Pong ball

PLAY BALL!

1 Hold the magazine upright so that it stands on the table. (It's the sail of a boat heading upwind toward you.)

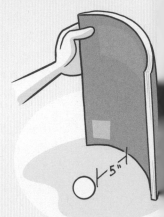

2 Curve the magazine slightly so that you're looking at the inside of the curve. It should look like a capital C if you look down on it from above, with the spine of the magazine pointing toward you.

3 Place the ball on the table about 5 inches out from the center of the magazine.

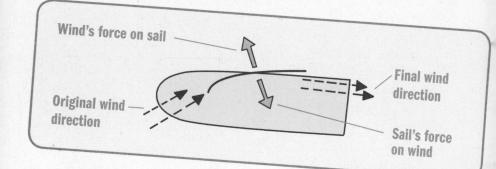

Wind's force on sail

Original wind direction

Final wind direction

Sail's force on wind

TWO-MINUTE WARNING You will probably need to fiddle with the angles to get this just right. But the payoff is worth it!

4 Crouch down so that your mouth is at table level and blow toward the inside of the curving magazine.

5 The ball should roll directly rightward from the magazine and not diagonally away from you as you might have expected.

SLO-MO REPLAY ▷

You just saw part of the action-reaction that helps power sailboats upwind. The ball was blown sharply rightward. And if you had enough strength in your breath, you would have seen the magazine billow up like a sail. But that's only part of the picture—otherwise a boat would be propelled, but diagonally. That's why they have deep keels (the piece that juts down from the bottom of the boat) to act as brakes against that diagonal motion. Once again, Newton shows up. With the billowing sail forcing the boat diagonally and the keel "reacting" equally, where can the boat go? Forward, of course!

Here's a bonus experiment: Imagine holding a marble between your thumb and forefinger—two forces like the sail and keel battling it out. Keep on squeezing, and the marble will shoot off, just like the boat!

SHOULDN'T IT BE EASIER FOR A KID TO "RIDE THE CURL"?

MAYBE YOU'VE SEEN SURFERS ON TELEVISION or even at the beach, riding the curls and pulling off some gnarly tricks. And perhaps you've tried some bodysurfing

yourself, hitching a ride for the last 30 feet of a righteous, foaming wave. So you're pretty annoyed when your older brother says you're too young to join him when he heads out to the breakers to go surfing. Pretty typical—he doesn't even give a good reason, let alone a scientific explanation! Hmm . . . maybe those laws of motion are on your side . . .

MASS MIX-UP

Here's the good news: It's way easier for younger people to ride smaller waves, which exert only enough force to propel a small mass (a child) and not enough to move a more massive person (an adult). But here's the bad news: Adults have a lower center of mass, making it easier to surf overall because they have better balance and maneuverability. Your center of mass gets lower as you grow up—our heads develop first (making us a little "top heavy") and then the rest of the body catches up. So the evidence might be against you, but here's how to show your brother that he might be better off on dry land while his girlfriend does all the surfing instead.

THE LINEUP

★ Kitchen chair

★ Wall

★ 2 adults (one man, one woman)

PLAY BALL!

 1 Place the chair with one side facing the wall.

2 Ask the man to go first. He should stand facing the wall, with his feet about a foot back from the side of the chair. Then, keeping his back flat, he should lean forward until his head touches the wall.

3 Staying in that "head against the wall" position, he should reach down with both arms, grasp the chair, and try to straighten up. It will be impossible.

TWO-MINUTE WARNING Make sure that the chair isn't too high—folding chairs (or similar-sized chairs) work well for this demonstration.

④ Set up the chair again and ask the woman to do Steps 2 and 3. She should be able to do it.

You've just seen an example of how the center of mass plays a big part in our lives. Men and women are shaped differently (*ahem!*), which affects where the center of mass is in someone's body. More of a woman's muscle tissue is located lower down, which lowers her center of mass compared to that of a man. So when the man leans forward, his center of mass is firmly over the chair, which makes it almost impossible for him to pick it up and straighten out again. The woman has her center of mass closer to her hips and still over her feet, making it easier to pick up the chair and straighten. So your brother's girlfriend has a center-of-mass advantage out on the waves—how do you think he'll take it?

HOW DO STONES SKIP?

SCIENCE EXPLAINS A HECKUVA LOT ABOUT our world. Many of the "big questions"—like why the Earth orbits the sun, how plants produce food from sunlight, or how fast the speed of light is—are all in the bag. But one seemingly simple activity has baffled our greatest thinkers for centuries: the science of skipping stones. Most of us have done it, or at least tried. Sometimes we've succeeded, getting four or five skips while wondering how the world champion ever managed to get 88. But whether it's a few skips, or close to a hundred, or just a big loud splash, what exactly is going on here?

ANGLE OF ATTACK

Here's what we do know: The stone hits the water with a downward force. The surface tension (chemical bonds that make the water surface stronger) prevents the stone from penetrating very far, and the water exerts an opposite and upward force (Newton's third law of motion). But that first hit (in scientific terms, a collision) wasn't perfectly elastic, and some of the kinetic (movement) energy of the stone was sent off in noise, splashing, and vibration—so it slows down a bit. Meanwhile, that flick of your wrist sent the stone spinning, which helped keep its near-level position into the next skip. But eventually the stone will lose that parallel position and dive right into the water.

The key to getting multiple skips is to use a flat stone and spin it really fast with lots of initial speed. But if you want to win next year's Stone Skimming Championships in Scotland (yes, it's real), you'll have to consider another element, one that French scientists who built a stone-skipping machine (yes, it's real, too) observed. You'll find out in this next experiment.

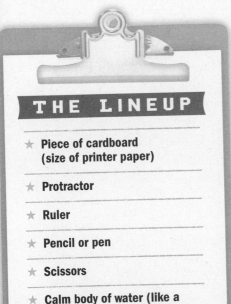

THE LINEUP

★ Piece of cardboard (size of printer paper)

★ Protractor

★ Ruler

★ Pencil or pen

★ Scissors

★ Calm body of water (like a lake, pond, bay, or harbor)

★ Flat stones weighing about 5 ounces (the weight of a medium-size apple)

★ Good throwing arm

PLAY BALL!

1 Lay the cardboard on a table and position the protractor at the bottom-left corner.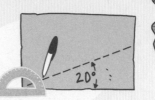

2 Make a mark at 20 degrees, remove the protractor, and use the ruler to draw a line from the corner to the mark and beyond.

3 Cut along that line and keep the cardboard with the 20-degree angle.

4 Go down to the water's edge and skip stones as you normally would. See the highest number you can make in five tries.

5 Now hold the cardboard upright at ground level at the water's edge and place a stone along the top edge: This will tell you what a 20-degree angle looks like as it approaches the water.

TWO-MINUTE WARNING Stone-skipping warnings? Come on, be serious! Well, go easy after about 15 or 20 throws. You can get a sore arm (just like a pitcher who's about to be yanked from the game). But you can always enlist help from friends who are in on the experiment.

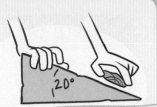

 Keep an image of that angle in your mind's eye; it will be hard to be precise, but try your best.

7 Now try five more throws, crouching low to the water as you throw and trying to match that 20-degree angle.

8 Try five throws each at different angles (some more, some less acute than 20 degrees) and observe which one produces the best results.

SLO-MO REPLAY ▶

Those French scientists tested all sorts of factors to find the highest skips: water temperature, air temperature, rate of spin, speed of throw, shape and weight of the stones. But the factor that outranked all of these was the "angle of attack." That's the angle at which the stone collides with the water surface. And the angle that produced the best results, hands down, was 20 degrees.

Angles less than 20 degrees let the stone carve into the water, often without a single skip. Angles greater than 20 degrees sent them flying up and back down too steeply, plunking into the water. The 20-degree skips managed to get a bounce (with the help of surface tension) while the angle remained shallow enough for the stone to continue its forward flight path. Check to see whether you agree with your French colleagues.

Why Does a BELLY FLOP HURT SO MUCH?

THE ONE-METER-HIGH DIVING BOARD AT THE local pool may look like a cakewalk, but it isn't heights making you think twice about jumping in. It's that really painful chest and stomach from last time you tried a dive, like the world's worst sunburn (including the redness) all

down your front. Why would you want to risk feeling *that* again? If only there were some way of working out what causes belly flops and how to prevent them. After all, Olympians dive from 5 and 10 meters, and you don't see many of them crying afterward. And what about those people in Acapulco, Mexico, who dive off 115-foot cliffs?

THE TENSION MOUNTS

Well, there's a lot of science behind a dive, but the crucial bit for "belly-flopology" is the nature of the water surface as you hit it. As you approach the water, your body has lots of kinetic (movement) energy. When you hit with a belly flop—and your motion stops suddenly—that kinetic energy turns into other forms of energy such as sound (the splashing noise), other kinetic energy (waves), and heat (the burning that you feel on your chest).

It's all down to the water surface and your point of entry. Chemical bonds strengthen the surface of the water so that a wide surface like your belly hits something that almost feels solid. A narrower point of entry, like your hands together, helps you "slice" through those bonds, so the dive doesn't hurt. Let's take a closer look— by the end of this experiment, you may be a certified belly-flopologist.

THE LINEUP

★ Mixing bowl

★ Paper clip

★ Paper towel or dish towel

★ Cold water

PLAY BALL!

 1 Fill the mixing bowl two-thirds with cold water.

 2 Hold the paper clip vertically over the mixing bowl and let it drop; it should sink straight down.

3 Remove the paper clip, dry it with the towel, and bend one of its arms so that it points straight up when the paper clip is lying on the table.

TWO-MINUTE WARNING It's important to ensure that the water has become calm again (Step 4) before you drop the paper clip for the second time. As a good scientist, you're trying to make sure that conditions are the same for both drops.

4 Wait until the water in the mixing bowl is calm and then hold the paper clip by the "handle" you created.

5 Lower the paper clip slowly until the body of the clip touches the water's surface. Let go, and it should float.

Surface tension—the condition that makes water feel almost solid when you hit it—is the result of a chemical process. Water is made up of hydrogen and oxygen atoms (that's why its chemical formula is H_2O). The hydrogen holds together with strong chemical bonds that become particularly strong when the water is calm. If you slide your hand in narrowly (or if a paper clip goes in vertically), those hydrogen bonds are eased apart. But if you "slap" the water side-on (or drop a "belly flopping" paper clip), then you're battling against a hydrogen wall—and you definitely know it when you hit it.

If you look closely at diving competitions, you'll see some water flowing into the pool, creating a few ripples—just enough to disrupt surface tension. So although the divers themselves usually enter the water at the best angle, at least the surface isn't like a brick wall if they're a little off-target.

AFTERWORD

Whether it's a football team's record winning streak, a gymnast's run of perfect 10s, or a tennis star's umpteenth ace at a Grand Slam tournament, many sports achievements can seem hard to explain. Is it lots of training and practice, or just simple luck that makes all the difference? Or have the preceding pages convinced you that something more, something a bit . . . *scientific* . . . could be a secret ingredient?

You might never make your way to the top of a mountain for your first ski jump, and you'd probably think twice about hurtling around a racetrack at 100 mph, or karate-chopping a stack of boards. But after reading this book you should have a better idea of how science is the foundation for those thrilling exploits. Better still, you should begin to harness some scientific principles for sports activities closer to home.

Bernoulli's principle helps send airplanes up—and keeps race cars down—but it also explains how curveballs and corner kicks work so well. It seems to make sense that a trampoline demonstrates an elastic collision, but now you'll know that a satisfying line drive in softball relies on the same bit of science. Newton's second law? Conservation of energy? Momentum? The list of scientific principles—and their sports counterparts—goes on and on.

And here's an unexpected bonus. One day you'll come across some of those scientific terms in science class. Let the others puzzle out what the Magnus effect or angular momentum are all about. You can allow yourself a slight smile as you nod and think about knuckleballs, spiral passes, and spinning figure skaters.

Who knows? Maybe you will have made yourself a little luck in school too. Have fun!

GLOSSARY

ACCELERATION A change in velocity, commonly referring to a change in speed.

AIR PRESSURE The force pressing on an object caused by the air (or the atmosphere).

AIR TURBULENCE Disruption caused when two air masses traveling at different speeds collide.

AIRFOIL A partly curved structure added to aircraft wings and the frame of other vehicles to direct the movement of air passing across it. Air traveling across the curved surface exerts less pressure, allowing air on the other side to push up (or down) more strongly.

ANGLE OF ATTACK The angle between oncoming wind and a flat object traveling through it.

ANGLE OF INCIDENCE The measure of the difference between perpendicular ("straight on") and the angle at which a moving object meets a surface.

ANGULAR MOMENTUM The momentum of an object traveling in a circle. The object's speed increases as it draws closer to the center of the spinning movement and decreases as it moves farther out from it.

AXIS OF ROTATION The imaginary straight line through all the points of a spinning object that form the center of the spinning. The Earth's axis of rotation runs from the North Pole all the way through to the South Pole.

BERNOULLI'S PRINCIPLE The pressure of a moving stream of fluid (liquid or gas) reduces as its speed increases.

BOYLE'S LAW The volume of a gas decreases as the pressure exerted on it increases, and vice versa.

CENTER OF MASS The point in an object (or group of objects) at which the mass is concentrated. It is sometimes called the center of gravity as a way to explain how some shapes remain balanced while others topple over.

CENTRIPETAL FORCE The force that pulls an object traveling in a circular path toward the center of that path.

COEFFICIENT OF FRICTION The measure of friction produced when one object moves across a surface.

COEFFICIENT OF RESTITUTION The measure of how much kinetic energy is retained when objects collide.

COLLISION A meeting of objects that leads to a transfer or exchange of energy.

CONSERVATION OF ENERGY The concept stating that the total amount of energy in an "isolated system" remains the same, although it can change form. It explains, for example, how the potential energy of someone climbing a diving board changes to kinetic energy when she dives off.

CONSERVATION OF MOMENTUM The concept stating that when two objects collide, the total amount of momentum of the two objects before the collision is the same as after the collision.

DRAG A force that is opposite to an object's motion, and which increases as the object's speed increases.

ELASTIC COLLISION A collision in which the total kinetic energy is preserved and not changed into other forms of energy.

EMPIRICAL STUDY An examination of a scientific concept or problem based on gathering evidence and drawing conclusions based on that evidence.

FLUID A substance, such as a liquid or gas, that is made of particles that can move freely without separating the mass of the substance.

FLUID DYNAMICS The study of the behavior of fluids and the forces that act on them.

FORCE The energy or power that causes movement.

FRICTION The force that resists or acts against the motion of one thing against another.

GLUCOSE A simple sugar that provides energy for many living organisms, including humans.

GRAVITY The physical force that draws objects toward each other.

GYROSCOPE A device that uses the property of angular momentum to remain spinning in the same place.

IMPULSE A change in momentum equal to the amount of force on an object multiplied by the amount of time a collision takes. Increasing the time decreases the force, such as when a soccer player traps a ball.

INELASTIC COLLISION A collision in which the total kinetic energy is turned into other forms of energy, such as heat or sound.

KINETIC ENERGY The force of an object caused by its movement.

LAMINAR FLOW The straight movement of a liquid or gas.

LEVER A simple machine consisting of a rigid bar resting on a fixed point (known as a fulcrum) and used to transmit force to an object at a second point by applying pressure to a third point. Pressing down on one end of a seesaw transmits an upward force to the other end. The crossbar hinge in the middle is the fulcrum.

LIFT The force acting to lift an object upward.

LINEAR MOMENTUM The momentum of an object traveling in a straight line.

LOFT The sending of an object high into the air in an arclike path.

MAGNUS EFFECT When air sticks to the edge of a spinning object and slows a little as it meets friction. That, in turn, causes the air on the other side to speed up and lose pressure because of Bernoulli's principle.

MASS A measure of how much matter is in an object. It is often measured by how much something weighs, but weight can change if there is a change in gravitational strength. For instance, a bowling ball would weigh less on the Moon (with its weaker gravity) though it would have the same mass as it did on Earth.

MOMENT ARM The distance of a lever arm from the axis of rotation. The longer the arm, the greater the force exerted at the other end.

MOMENT OF INERTIA A value given to the way in which mass is distributed around the axis of rotation. If the mass is spread farther from that axis, an object will be less easy to rotate. A golf putter whose head juts out on both sides of the shaft (the rotational axis) will be steadier and less likely to rotate when it strikes the ball.

MOMENTUM The measurement of mass in motion. The momentum of an object is equal to its mass multiplied by its velocity.

MUSCLE MEMORY The ability to repeat a bodily movement easily because the body's instructions to produce that movement have become familiar through practice.

NEWTON'S FIRST LAW A law of motion stating that an object at rest (motionless) will remain at rest unless an outside force acts on it. Likewise, a moving object will retain its velocity unless an outside force acts on it.

NEWTON'S SECOND LAW A law of motion stating that an object's force is equal to its mass multiplied by its acceleration.

NEWTON'S THIRD LAW A law of motion stating that for every action there is an opposite and equal reaction.

POTENTIAL ENERGY Stored energy that is the result of an object's position. A roller coaster climbing slowly has lots of potential energy, which transfers into kinetic energy when it starts to rush downhill.

PRESSURE A measure of how much force is acting over an area.

PRONATION A twisting motion of the hand or forearm so that the palm winds up pointing downward or toward the back.

PROPORTIONAL Having a direct and consistent mathematical connection, as when more force is needed to move an object with greater mass.

PSI An abbreviation for a measure of air pressure inside an inflated object (like a football or bike inner tube); stands for "pounds per square inch."

RADIUS The distance from the center of a circle (or spinning object) to the curve itself, or to the surface of the object.

RATIO A simple comparison of quantities with the same unit of measure.

SIMPLE MACHINE Any one of the basic mechanisms for transferring energy, usually including the lever, wheel and axle, pulley, wedge, inclined plane, and screw.

SURFACE AREA The overall space taken up by the exposed area of an object.

SURFACE TENSION A force causing the molecules of a liquid to be pushed together to form a resistant layer.

TORQUE A force that produces rotation.

TRANSFER OF ENERGY The term describing how energy shifts from one form to another.

UPDRAFT An upward-moving air current that helps aircraft stay aloft.

VELOCITY The measurement of the speed and direction of a moving object.

WAKE The track left by a moving object as it passes through a fluid.

PHOTO CREDITS

Alamy Stock Photo: epa european pressphoto agency b.v., p. 145; Nicholas Eveleigh, p. 64; Image Source, p. 168; Juice Images, p. 187; Yuri Kevhiev, p. 169 (broken egg); LAMB, pp. 166–167; Matt Perrin, p. 198; photostock1, pp. 138–139; Pure Stock, pp. 136–137; SuperStock, p. 155. **Fotolia:** 31moonlight31, p. 196 (ice cubes); 3drenderings, p. 10; abhbah05, p. 28; Alekss, pp. 38, 212; alexzaitsev, pp. 222–223; alswart, pp. 83, 148–149, 151; anatchant, pp. 66, 205, 206, 212 (golf ball); jovica antoski, p. 50; Tony Baggett, p. 65; BillionPhotos.com, pp. 4, 12; Ionescu Bogdan, pp. 129, 130–131; Boggy, p. 204 (golf tees); Stepan Bormotov, pp. 94, 95; Chris Brignell, pp. 16, 18 (softball); Cla78, pp. 30, 31; davidsonlentz, p. 202; De Visu, p. 220; Dimitrius, p. 173; donatas1205, p. 128; Sergey Drozdov, p. 158 (cheetah); Emmoth, p. 66; fotopak, pp. 16, 18 (bat); Friday, p. 224; gekaskr, p. 41; giadophoto, pp. 66, 217, 219 (marbles); Lukas Gojda, p. 106 (skier); Gorilla, pp. 110–111 (mountain); Haslam Photography, p. 43; indigolotos, p. 77 (cue stick); IntelWond, pp. 39, 104, 105, 167, 169 (egg); jonnysek, pp. 98, 99, 100, 104 (snowflake); lazyllama, p. 68 (gymnast rings); Pavel Losevsky, p. 160 (hang glider left); madgooch, p. 76; mareandmare, pp. 10–11; Marek, p. 114; Sky Masterson, p. 78 (cue stick); mtsaride, pp. 26, 33, 34, 35; Dmitry Naumov, p. 122; nortongo, p. 196 (chopsticks); Tatyana Nyshko, p. 132 (bike left); phanlop88, p. 48; photology1971, p. 160 (hang glider right); photomelon, pp. 3, 7, 13, 17, 21, 27, 31, 35, 39, 43, 49, 53, 57, 61, 65, 69, 73, 77, 83, 87, 91, 95, 99, 103, 107, 111, 115, 119, 123, 129, 133, 137, 141, 145, 149, 153, 157, 161, 165, 171, 175, 179, 185, 191, 195, 199, 203, 207, 211, 217, 221, 225, 229, 233 (clipboard); picsfive, pp. 176–177; pzphotos, p. 34 (deflated football); Robbic, pp. 39, 66, 192, 194 (tennis balls); ronniechua, p. 52; rufar, p. 228 (stones); sarapon, p. 210 (putter right); silverspiralarts, pp. 2, 3, 6, 7, 11 (baseball); steheap, pp. 224–225; suradech14, p. 156; sveta, p. 178–179; Winai Tepsuttinun, pp. 76, 78 (cue ball); Tritooth, p. 42, 44; Dmitry Veryovkin, p. 90; VIPDesign, p. 68 (parallel bars); VITAMIN, p. 120; vladstar, p. 132; volkovslava, p. 158 (sneakers); WayneG, p. 2; westmarmaros, p. 117; wolfelarry, p. 190; ygor28, p. 14. **Getty Images:** Don Arnold/WireImage, p. 126; artcyclone/DigitalVision Vectors, p. 210 (golf putter middle); Atomic Imagery/Digital Vision, p. 88; Thomas Barwick/ Taxi, pp. 226–227; Bettmann, p. 102; Aurelie and Morgan David de Lossy/ Cultura, p. 232; George Diebold/The Image Bank, p. 20, 22; Jon Feingersh/ Blend Images, p. 170; Tim Graham, p. 183; Samir Hussein/WireImage, p. 182; Image Source, p. 144; JazzIRT/E+, pp. 188, 186; Petit Philippe/ Paris Match Archive, p. 216; Photodisc, p. 152; Peter Sebastian/The Image Bank, p. 184 (Frisbee right); Mayte Torres/Moment p. 164; walik/E+, pp. 83, 86, 118; wwing/E+, p. 210 (golf putter left); Charlie Yacoub/Stone, p. 174. **Shutterstock:** ayakovlevcom, p. 72; F8 studio, p. 60; Anna Jurkovska, p. 56; kontur-vid, p. 106 (skis); Kostsov, pp. 98, 110; Michael Rosskothen, p. 70; Stefan Schurr, 140; Boris Sosnovyy, p. 82.

GENIUS AT WORK!

More Books by
SEAN CONNOLLY

Sixty-four amazing science experiments that snap, crackle, pop, ooze, crash, boom, and stink! Giant air cannons. Matchbox microphones. They require no special training, use stuff from around the house, and demonstrate scientific principles like osmosis and Newton's third law of motion.

Perform 18 experiments adapted from Sean Connolly's bestseller. Includes a book with step-by-step instructions, plus a lateral split-orb measuring spoon, a vacuumatic test tube, a matter-retaining measuring cup, and photon-refracting goggles.

Fifty awesome experiments that allow kids to understand 34 of the greatest scientific breakthroughs in history. Using common household ingredients, the curious can now boldly go where the bravest scientists have gone before.

Math rocks! At least it does in the gifted hands of Sean Connolly, who blends middle school math with fantasy to create exciting adventures in problem-solving. The 24 problems challenge readers on fractions, algebra, geometry, and more.